Key Steps in Local Church Planning

Key Steps in Local Church Planning

Richard E. Rusbuldt • Richard K. Gladden • Norman M. Green, Jr.

From the
**LOCAL CHURCH
PLANNING MANUAL**

Judson Press ® Valley Forge

Key Steps in Local Church Planning
Copyright © 1980
Judson Press, Valley Forge, PA 19481

Unless otherwise indicated, Bible quotations in this volume are from Today's English Version, the *Good News Bible*—Old Testament: Copyright © American Bible Society, 1976; New Testament: Copyright © American Bible Society, 1966, 1971 1976. Used by permission

Library of Congress Cataloging in Publication Data

Rusbuldt, Richard E.
  Key steps in local church planning.

    Condensation of the authors' Local church planning manual.
    1. Church management—Handbooks, manuals, etc. I. Rusbuldt, Richard E. Local church planning manual. II. Gladden, Richard K., joint author. III. Green, Norman M., joint author. IV. Title.
BV652.R872   254   80-12610
ISBN 0-8170-0881-0

The name JUDSON PRESS is registered as a trademark in the U.S. Patent Office.
Printed in the U.S.A.

Preface

"Local churches have long asked for help in planning."

These words begin our 248-page *Local Church Planning Manual,* or LCPM as it has become nicknamed (Judson Press, 1977). The LCPM was our first attempt to help answer the request. Now that it is well into the sale of its second printing, many of its purchasers have made another request. They have asked us to prepare a mini-edition, a smaller volume which could be used alone or in company with the larger book.

As requested, this mini-edition is a digest of the LCPM's key parts.

Key Steps in Local Church Planning is an introduction to and an overview of planning, a companion for the LCPM. All phases of planning are treated, but without the detailed examples and worksheets carried in our first book. What have been eliminated are the resources primarily required by those who have accepted the responsibility for guiding and coordinating the planning procedures in a local church.

Key Steps in Local Church Planning has been designed for:
  (1) persons who wish to explore what is involved in careful, intentional planning;
  (2) persons who wish to be responsible participants in planning;
  (3) groups or congregations small enough to permit the kinds of face-to-face contacts which do not require the organization for planning often necessary in larger congregations.

As authors, we continue to be indebted to persons acknowledged in the preface to the *Local Church Planning Manual.* Moreover, since its publication, our wives—to whom the LCPM was dedicated—have continued unabated their devotion and support which undergird all phases of our ministries. Our gratitude to them, along with our wonder and amazement at their patient forbearance, has likewise increased! They and we join in dedicating this volume to our next generation:

Diane	Rebecca	Russell
Melody	Susan	Cynthia
Richard	John	Sharon
Dawn	Kathryn	Deona
David		

Richard E. Rusbuldt • Richard K. Gladden • Norman M. Green, Jr.
Valley Forge, Pennsylvania • September, 1979

Contents

Introduction

Luke tells us that early in his ministry, Jesus took the Isaiah scroll and read the following words to the worshipers in Nazareth:
"The Spirit of the Lord is upon me,
because he has chosen me to
bring good news to the poor.
He has sent me to proclaim
liberty to the captives
and recovery of sight to the blind,
to set free the oppressed
and announce that the time has come
when the Lord will save his people."
(Luke 4:18-19, TEV)

He used these words to describe the way he would minister.

Later, Jesus called twelve disciples, trained and taught them, and sent them out. He encouraged his disciples by saying they would do even greater works than he (John 14:12).

Your church's ministry comes directly from what Jesus handed on to his disciples.

This book is designed to help churches decide how they can best carry out what Christ is calling them to do. It can be a tool for helping persons respond to the leading of the Holy Spirit. This book, by showing how to plan together, can help persons cooperate as agents of God's will.

"Churches are sometimes like people. Some are lazy; others are

9

hard working. Some look for Christ's direction; others ignore Christ's leadership. Some think and pray and plan; others sit and argue and fail."[1]

> If you don't know (or care)
> *where* you're going, *how* (or
> if) you get there doesn't
> matter.

There are three reasons for planning: (1) to know *where* you're going, (2) to figure out *how* to get there, (3) to know *when* you have arrived.

Planning is a way to think about tomorrow; so when tomorrow becomes today, we can be ready. Churches that plan put aside thoughts of "do what you can and hope for the best." They challenge and claim the future with confidence. Such planning can bring new vitality to the mission of a local church.

What Is Planning?

Planning is a discipline. Planning is a process. Planning has "steps" in it. Following the steps of planning is a good way to make better decisions. A good planning process will help your church discover *who* it is and *what* it is, decide *what* it should do, *how* it should do what it does, and *when*. Further, planning will help your church know how well it achieved what it wanted to accomplish.

Why Should Your Church Plan?

Perhaps you've heard others give reasons for *not* planning.[2]

> Plans are out-of-date almost as soon as they are written down.

> No one knows what tomorrow will bring—maybe opportunities, maybe disasters.

---

[1] W. L. Howse and W. O. Thomason, *A Church Organized and Functioning* (Nashville: Convention Press, 1963), p. 8.

[2] Adapted from "Why Plan?" by Jeffry A. Timmons and John L. Hayes, appearing in *New Venture Creation* by Jeffry A. Timmons, Leonard E. Smollen, and Alexander L. M. Dingee, Jr. (Homewood, Ill.: Richard D. Irwin, Inc., 1977), chapter 6; used with the authors' permission.

You can't predict the future; it's dangerous today to decide about tomorrow.

We can't afford the time planning takes.

The chances are that people said the same thing to Noah while he was building the ark! Now, here are some reasons *for* planning:

1. The steps of disciplined planning provide more decision points in a church's life and give the Holy Spirit more opportunities to lead us.

2. Volunteers do much of the work of a church; systematic planning helps to identify, enlist, and organize volunteers for ministry.

3. Planning helps persons to work *smarter* rather than *harder*. Planning helps us find better ways by forcing us to consider alternatives.

4. Planning encourages us to think about the future. Thinking ahead helps us be more alert to problems, opportunities, and changes that affect what we do.

5. Planning develops "keener" programs by testing the ideas of a few by the judgments of many. (Planning helps avoid the problem of only one or two persons making the decisions.)

6. The efforts people invest in a planning process build momentum to work toward common goals and related objectives. Planning helps people to know just what it is they are being asked to do.

7. Planning helps us pay attention to the results we get because of what we did. It lets us avoid simply being "busy." In short, planning provides the basis for evaluation.[3]

8. Planning can build a foundation of support. Being involved in decisions about "what to do" and "how to do" gets church members thinking and gives them a chance to "buy in" early, when their thinking can make a difference.

---

[3] *Ibid.*, for reasons 3-7.

What Must Your Church Have in Order to Plan?

First, the leaders of your church (including your pastor) must believe that a planning process will help you work better as a group. They must be willing to learn how to plan. And, most of all, they must be willing to follow the discipline of the planning steps.

Planning is hard work! It is no simple shortcut to the future. In fact, the first time a church moves through a planning process, it will probably find some members saying that planning is demanding and consumes a lot of time. They will be right. "The first experience of planning in a thorough manner may well be somewhat miserable and agonizing; a frustrating experience."[4] However, those who have worked at planning have seen dead churches come alive, listless people find new energy for the Lord's work, the quality of stewardship increase, and church administration become more effective—more ministry for the money.

This book can help your church look at why you exist (your purpose) and work out specific day-to-day ministries to accomplish goals and/or objectives necessary for you to be faithful to your purpose.

Successful planning experiences bear witness that planning is worth the investment of time, patience, and dollars. To plan well, you will need motivated church leaders who are willing to look toward the future and to include the participation of those who are concerned about the present.

---

[4] *Ibid.*

An Overview of the Planning Process

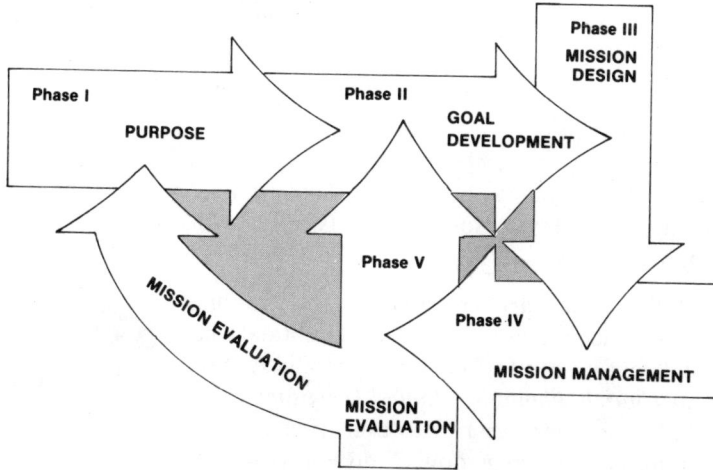

This planning process guides you step by step to say who you are, to define where you are going, to describe how you will get there, and to be aware of how far you have gone. It will also help you know how to be effective in the future by applying what you find out along the way.

Each of the five interlocking arrows in the diagram represents a Phase in the planning process.

Phase I Purpose—reviewing what your church is called to be and to become.

Phase II Goal Development—creating goals and objectives based on your purpose in light of all you can learn about your church, your community, and the world.

Phase III Mission Design—designing program plans and their details as the means for working toward an objective.

Phase IV Mission Management—doing the ministry of the church according to program plan details.

Phase V Mission Evaluation—drawing conclusions and making recommendations based on collected facts about what you did and what happened as a result.

Churches will require different lengths of time for the first three phases. We urge you to complete Phases I, II, and III within twelve months of the time you begin your planning. Pace your planning to take account of vacation periods (winter or summer) for your planning leaders.

Problems may arise as you use this planning process. A helpful tool, "Why Plans Fail" (and what to do about it), can be found in Appendix K of the *Local Church Planning Manual* (hereafter called LCPM in all references).[5] However, if your whole planning process "bogs down," do not hesitate to get outside assistance (look to your denomination for help).

At the time of publication, this book is the "latest" word in church planning. It is not the last word. As with everything, this resource can be improved by additional experiences. You, the reader, are requested to send us, the authors (in care of Judson Press), any comments and suggestions arising from your experience with *Key Steps in Local Church Planning*.

---

[5] Richard E. Rusbuldt, Richard K. Gladden, Norman M. Green, Jr., *Local Church Planning Manual* (Valley Forge: Judson Press, 1977).

Definitions

Area Minister—The denominational staff person responsible for churches in your geographical area (page 29).

Areas of Concern—Something about your church life, your community, or the world that calls you to act because of the way your church has stated its purpose and assumptions (page 50).

Assumption—What you believe to be true and are willing to act upon; makes you confident even when you lack complete information; is your judgment of what the available facts mean; is the foundation upon which your church's goals, objectives, and program plans rest (pages 43-44).

Data—Facts, statistics, or the like, either from historical records or produced by asking questions, observing, or testing (pages 38-41).

Environmental Assumptions—What you believe to be true about your community and the world (the contexts in which you live). Environmental assumptions should describe your town or city, county, and state, as well as the worldwide situations that could both affect and be affected by your congregation (pages 47-48).

Evaluation—The act of considering carefully the worth or value of what has happened as a result of your planning (page 89).

Goal—A statement expressing a condition or "end-state" you wish to attain, a desired long-range result of ministry (page 56).

Information—An organized body of data; knowledge produced by putting data into some order and interpreting it (page 42).

Information Summary—The report in which many pieces of data are organized by agreed-upon categories. Data pieces, when related to each other and when examined carefully for meanings, can become usable information (page 42).

Objective—A clear, simple statement of a target to be reached, it is derived from a goal statement. It should be stated in such a way that movement toward achieving the goal to which it is related can be measured (page 64).

Operational Assumption—What you believe to be true about your church's traditions, organization, and ways of operating (how it goes about doing its work); what you believe about its present and future strengths and weaknesses (pages 48-49).

Phase—One of the five major clusters of planning activities (page 13).

Planning Task Force—The persons named to direct your planning (pages 32-34).

Program Coordinator—That person who coordinates all aspects of the planned programs for your church and through whom your Program Plan Managers report to the Planning Task Force (pages 85-87).

Program Plan—A blueprint describing in general how to use what you have to achieve each objective (pages 74-77).

Program Plan Details—The individual parts of a Program Plan (page 77).

Program Plan Manager—The person responsible for a Program Plan from its early stages through evaluation (pages 84-85).

Purpose—The general, comprehensive long-range reason(s) why your church should continue to exist (page 21).

Purpose Statement—A clear, concise description of the purpose of your church in terms of what it is to be rather than what it is to do (page 22).

Step—One of the necessary planning activities within each of the five phases listed on page 13.

Theological Assumptions—What you believe to be true about what God *because of God's nature* is calling the people of God to do *because of their nature* (pages 46-47).

Points of Entry
to Planning

You, the reader (whether lay or clergy), must decide who in your church should also become familiar with this planning process. If you are a layperson, invite your pastor to study planning with you. If you are a pastor, share this material with the lay leaders who can help you make church planning work.

You can begin *long-range planning* at two points and *program planning* at another.

Entry A▷ (Long-range Planning) Begin by studying your *church's purpose*. We strongly recommend this approach since a study of your church's purpose is basic to determining what you hope to accomplish.

Some church members may not be ready to start planning by

discussing purpose. They may not immediately see this as a need. Or, they may feel more secure to begin planning by looking at what they are already doing. In this case use Entry B.

Entry B >   Begin with Step 2:1 in the *Goal Development* Phase of
(Long-range   the planning model. (This step is called "Form a
Planning)   Planning Task Force.") As you work through
Step 2:2 ,   Step 2:3 , and Step 2:4 , you will find it important at some point to return to the purpose section (referred to in Entry A) and complete that task before trying to write your church goals.

    The option available for church program planners is to use the work done by an already existing Planning Task Force to move directly into Program Plans.

Entry C >   Program planners can enter the planning process by
(Program   starting with Step 2:8 of Goal Development,
Planning)   "Write Goals." Those responsible for each program
           (youth ministry, women's work, social concern, evangelism, etc.) should ask the Planning Task Force for the church's purpose statement and for any statistical and/or other information that has been gathered and reduced to "Areas of Concern."

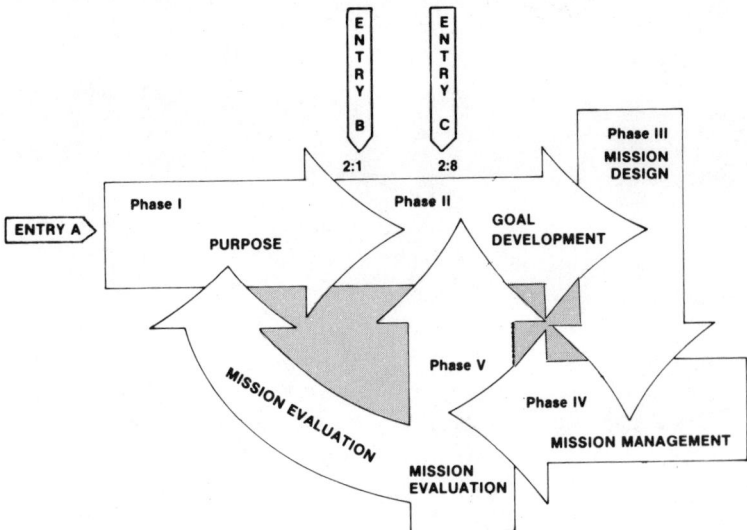

Said Alice to the Cheshire cat,
"Which way shall I go?"

Said the cat,
"Where do you want to go?"

"I don't really know," answered Alice.

I don't really know!

"Then," said the cat, "if you don't know where you want to go, it doesn't much matter which way you go, does it?"

BUT FOR US IT DOES MATTER—

... For Christ's Church ...
... And particularly for your local church ...

Phase I
The Purpose of Your Church

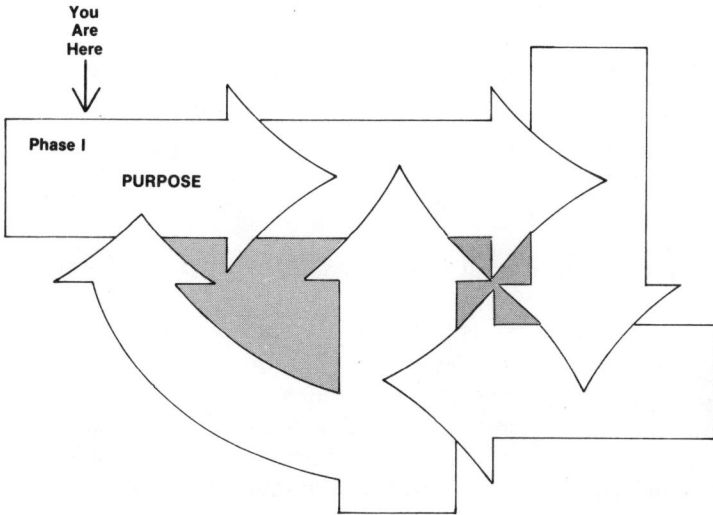

**You
Are
Here**

Phase I

PURPOSE

INTRODUCTION

**STEP
1:0**   Effective ministry is more likely to happen when church members are aware of and thoroughly familiar with the church's "reasons for being." Everything you do (programs, ministries, stewardship, etc.) should begin with and reflect your church's stated purpose.

Purpose: The general, comprehensive, long-range reason(s) why your church should continue to exist.

Why consider the purpose of your congregation? The first step in planning is to understand why your organization exists: what it feels it should become, or, in other words, what it must *be* to justify its existence.

A clear purpose statement *sets the stage* for all your church should do. The purpose statement becomes the basis for setting priorities, choosing programs and projects, evaluating results. A purpose statement which uses vague generalizations or which dodges issues can cripple planning. On the other hand, a clear purpose statement can focus attention and energies for action.

A clearly stated church purpose statement:

1. *Can help persons think biblically and/or theologically;*
2. *Can help persons think about the world in which they minister;*
3. *Can help persons think about how their church operates or, perhaps, should operate.*

Does working on a purpose statement have to take a lot of time? That depends. Some planning committees, using only a few sessions, have refined their church's purpose statement so it could be given to the congregation for review and vote. On the other hand, *reviewing-and-revising* or *writing* a purpose statement can represent three or four months of hard work. For this reason some congregations decide to carry on business as usual for several months while their planning group works to clarify the purpose statement.

Most churches have a purpose statement (or a statement of mission), usually found in their constitutions or official church documents. If not found elsewhere, every incorporated church will find a purpose statement in its Articles of Incorporation.

> If your church does not have a purpose statement, your task is clear—prepare one as your foundation for planning.
> Begin with Steps 1:1 , 1:2 , and 1:3 . Next, go to Step 1:6 and continue the process.
> When you get to Step 1:9 , follow Route 3.

How to Begin Planning by Working on Your Purpose Statement . . .

SELECT A PURPOSE STATEMENT
WRITING GROUP

STEP 1:1

The first step is to name a purpose statement writing group. The group should represent the total congregation and include:

—church members who have a strong commitment to Christ and your church

—church members who are willing to invest time and energy in a process that could take several months

—a cross section of your congregation, such as college youths, single-parent families, elderly living alone, shift workers, etc.

—persons who tend to reflect on the "good old days" as well as persons who tend to look forward to change

—a chairperson with the ability to lead the group in writing a purpose statement.

Purpose writing should be a group operation, with the pastor present but not dominating. There is no better place for your minister to give assistance in planning than as your theologian-in-residence. The pastor's job here, however, is not to do the group's thinking. Your pastor should introduce issues, provide helpful resources, and suggest procedures for working on your purpose statement.

A church purpose statement can be written by either an existing or a newly created group. Consider the following approaches. Choose the one that seems to fit your church best.

1. Form *a special task force,* representative of the congregation, to prepare your purpose statement.

2. Use *an already existing group,* such as a church board, council, committee, or some other representative group.

3. If your church has *a one-board structure,* use that board as a total group or form a purpose statement task force from among its membership.

4. If your church has a *two-board structure,* create a task force of representatives from both boards.

5. A church with *a three (or more)-board structure* can use a modification of #4.

6. If your congregation has already decided to use systematic

planning and has already named a *Planning Task Force,* use that task force.[1]

Whichever approach you choose, the group should follow the steps in Phase I. Step 1:2 is important to help your congregation understand the task your group is undertaking.

SERMON SUPPORT

STEP
1:2

During the time you work on your purpose statement, ask your pastor to deliver several sermons that deal with "The importance of a church's purpose being up-to-date and vital so it can guide planning for the future." Ask your pastor *not* to preach on your church's current purpose statement; this will be dealt with later. You can begin Step 1:3 immediately.

YOUR CHURCH'S HISTORY

STEP
1:3

Distribute to your purpose-statement writing group a brief, up-to-date history of your church.

If you do not have one, write a brief history of your church. Ask someone who has been around a while to outline the history; feature significant events, specific ministries, services to the community, and accomplishments. The history should touch only the highlights. More can be studied and written later. Give a copy to every member of your group.

As You Begin Actual Work on a Purpose Statement . . .

ANSWER SOME QUESTIONS ABOUT CONGREGATIONAL AWARENESS

STEP
1:4

In what areas does your church function? It probably worships, proclaims, educates, and ministers (serves others). You may see additional functions. Does most of what you do as a congregation reflect your purpose? How well do your members know your stated purpose? Ask your group to answer the following questions:

1. Do more than 50 percent of your church members know you have a statement of purpose?

Yes_____ No_____

---

[1] See pages 32-33 for criteria to form a Planning Task Force.

2. Have your elected leaders studied your statement of purpose within the last two years?

Yes_____ No_____

3. If your congregation has specific goals, are these related to your purpose statement?

Yes_____ No_____

4. Does your church's budget-raising activity take account of your purpose statement?

Yes_____ No_____

"Yes" answers suggest your congregation is probably aware of what your church has in the past said is its reason for being (its purpose). "No" answers suggest your congregation may be unaware that you even have a stated purpose. The next task is to examine your purpose statement by moving to Step 1:5 .

STUDY YOUR STATEMENT OF PURPOSE

STEP 1:5   Ask each member of your group to examine your church's statement of purpose and answer the following questions:

1. How recently has it been revised?
2. What does each phrase or clause in the purpose statement mean to *me?*
3. Is it relevant for today?
4. Can our church move toward what the purpose statement implies?
5. Do current church programs directly reflect our purpose statement?
6. Does the statement reflect what our congregation really wants to be?
7. Does our congregation seem to have a future ministry in terms of what its purpose statement implies?
8. What does the purpose statement suggest our congregation should do which no other community or business groups are likely to do? What difference does the statement imply our congregation should make in our community?

STUDY SCRIPTURES TOGETHER

| STEP 1:6 | The Bible says helpful things about the purposes of the Church. It says the Church is a fellowship, a called-out community, the people of God, the body of Christ. You |

are a part of that Church. Read some of the following passages privately. Discuss the implications for your congregation. If you feel a Scripture passage says little to you, your church, or your group, move to another passage.

1. Exodus 3:13-17 and Matthew 28:18-20—Two "Great Commission" Scriptures
2. Isaiah 53—"The Suffering Servant"
3. Jeremiah 7:1-15—"This Is the Temple of the LORD"
4. Esther 4:14—"For Such a Time As This"
5. Mark 8:27-38—"We See and Yet Do Not Understand"
6. John 3:16-20—"The Object of God's Love"
7. John 8:31-36—"The Truth Will Make You Free"
8. John 10:7-18—"I Came That They May Have Life"
9. Romans 12:1-21—"Christian Style of Life"
10. 1 Corinthians 12:4-31—"All Members of One Body"
11. 2 Corinthians 5:16-21—"Ministry of Reconciliation"
12. Ephesians 1:1-23—"The Lordship of Christ"
13. Ephesians 4:1-16—"Christ's Gifts"
14. 1 John 2:7-11—"The Test Is Love"

Note: The Bible does not "prepackage" church purpose statements. Instead, in the Bible God gives suggestions to help us discover the purpose for each congregation's unique situation. Other Scripture passages are listed in Appendix D in LCPM.

| STEP 1:7 | (An optional exercise carried on page 23 of LCPM.) |

STUDY EXTREMES IN PURPOSE STATEMENTS

| STEP 1:8 | The way you write your purpose statement will determine the direction and style of ministry for your church. A purpose statement should help your congrega- |

tion discover what should be done and provide the "push" to get it done. *How* you state your purpose is important.

Consider this sample purpose statement, "X":

> The purpose of this church, as the body of Christ in close and loving fellowship, is to maintain the holy worship of God and the spiritual nurture of our members.

This statement says that *worship for its members, a close-knit fellowship,* and *maintenance* of local church life are important. The statement will lead the church to focus on its internal life.

Consider this sample purpose statement, "Y":

> The purpose of our church is to witness to all persons that Jesus Christ, Lord and Savior, calls us to hear and to respond as His servants in the midst of human life, in the places where we work and spend our days.

This statement says the congregation should *involve itself in depth in its community* and in "other-than-local-church" concerns. The statement will *not* lead the church to maintain its support base, the local church itself.

Neither of these sample purpose statements is adequate because each represents an extreme position. Your purpose statement should provide a balance in what it emphasizes.

STOP HERE!
Three routes are
now open to you...

WHICH ROUTE TO FOLLOW?

| STEP 1:9 | STOP HERE! Three routes are now open to you: **Route 1)** Submit your purpose statement in its present form to your official board or congregation. |

Route 2) Revise or modify your present purpose statement; then submit it to the official board or congregation.

Route 3) Write a new purpose statement which can be submitted to your official board or congregation.

Now, choose either **Route 1, Route 2,** or **Route 3.** If you select **Route 1,** move to ⬚Step 1:11⬚ . If you select **Route 2** or **Route 3,** move to ⬚Step 1:10⬚ .

REVISE, REWRITE, OR WRITE YOUR PURPOSE STATEMENT

| STEP 1:10 |

Put into simple, direct sentences why your church exists—*TODAY.* After developing a first draft statement, your group may want to set its work aside for a week or so to let it cool off before coming together to work on it again. Time away from the product of creative group work often helps understanding. It gives each group member an opportunity to think things through alone.

Guidelines for writing a purpose statement:[2]

1. Answer some basic questions:
    a. Why should your church continue to exist?
    b. Why do you conduct worship services, church school classes, youth programs, etc.?
    c. What should your church *be* as a part of the body of Christ?
2. Make sure your purpose statement deals with the vertical relationship between your church and God.
3. Confine your thinking to *basic* reasons why your church exists, rather than including specific programs, services, or ministries. These will be dealt with later.
4. Strive for quality and honesty; do not be overly concerned if you feel you do not have a perfect purpose statement. As you gain more experience in planning, you will become more expert in stating your church's purpose. (The purpose statement can be reviewed at the end of the evaluation, Phase V ⬚Step 5:5⬚ .)

NOTE! If your group has difficulty in developing its purpose statement, get some help. Do not hesitate to ask your area

---

[2] If needed, you will find several examples of purpose statements in Appendix C of LCPM. Mentioning them does not in any way suggest that these could or should be used by your church; they are offered only as suggestions to stimulate your thinking.

minister,[3] other denominational staff, or resource persons in your community to assist you. This is a critical step! Don't give up!

SEEK REACTIONS

| STEP 1:11 | When you have completed your draft of the purpose statement, we suggest you review the statement in light of Step 1:8 . Then, refer it to your area minister or |

other resource person for reaction and counsel. Consider what this person says as you prepare your final draft.

ADOPT AND REFER YOUR STATEMENT

| STEP 1:12 | Keep working on the statement until your group is satisfied with the way it is worded. Take time to revise or rewrite until agreement is reached. |

When your group has agreed on the statement it wants to refer, forward that statement to the appropriate board or council for consideration. Supply any background information needed to explain the process you used to develop the statement.

PRESENTING THE PROPOSED PURPOSE STATEMENT

| STEP 1:13 | The purpose statement, once approved by the appropriate board or council, should be submitted to your congregation for discussion, modification (if necessary), |

and action to accept or reject.[4] Some denominations do not require congregational approval of policy. However, all churches will find it helpful in planning to take this step.

AFTER APPROVAL

| STEP 1:14 | Three things should happen NEXT. 1. *Communicate the purpose statement.* Use all available methods and media to communicate the |

purpose statement to your members on a continuing basis. For

---

[3] The denominational staff person responsible for churches in your geographical area.

[4] If the congregation should happen not to accept the purpose statement, your group can do one of two things: (1) it can "go back to the drawing board" and try again, or (2) it can ask to be dismissed with appreciation so another group can be named to carry on the work.

example, your purpose statement can be the subject for an adult elective course in your church school; it can be used for small group study; every class held for new members should contain some study of purpose; a set of slides on your church's purpose can be prepared for use by classes, organizations, committees, boards, etc.

2. *Use the purpose statement in preaching.* After the purpose statement is adopted, your pastor should be invited to deliver several sermons on it, laying groundwork for continuing the planning process. One way would be to use a full month when the new purpose statement is the subject of the Sunday morning sermons. The first sermon could be the responsibility of the pastor; the second could be assigned to a laywoman or layman; the third could be assigned to another layperson (of the opposite sex from the previous person), and the fourth sermon again by the pastor.

3. *Use the purpose statement in planning.* As you move through this planning process, when it is called for, use your purpose statement.

Phase II
Goal Development

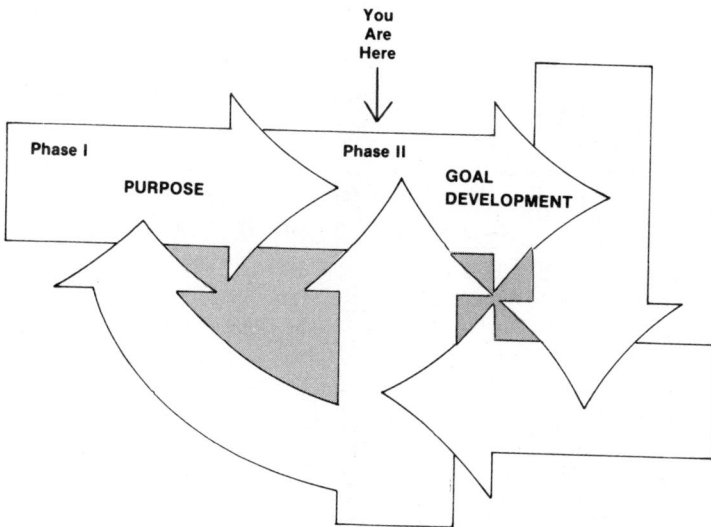

You
Are
Here

Phase I

PURPOSE

Phase II

**GOAL
DEVELOPMENT**

INTRODUCTION

**STEP
2:0**

Once you have an approved Purpose Statement, you are ready to move to Goal Development, the second phase of the planning process. There are ten steps in Goal Development:

Step 2:1   Form a Planning Task Force
Step 2:2   Look at Your Present Situation
Step 2:3   Gather Data About Your Church, Community, and World

Step 2:4   Prepare an Information Summary
Step 2:5   Compare Your Feelings and Facts
Step 2:6   List Your Assumptions
Step 2:7   Identify Needs and Concerns
Step 2:8   Write Goals
Step 2:9   Write Objectives
Step 2:10 Set Priorities Among Objectives

The chairperson, your pastor, and other Planning Task Force members should become familiar with all ten steps prior to your first meeting. It may be possible for you to make some advance assignments, particularly ⬚Step 2:3⬚ , to speed up the gathering of data. If you do this, be sure to brief all task force members on the content of ⬚Step 2:3⬚ and the reason for the advance assignments.

Involving many persons in the planning process multiplies opportunities for "ownership" on the part of all church members. Encourage your members to provide input; involve as many persons as possible in ⬚Step 2:3⬚ , the data-gathering step.

The planning decisions you make as you follow this process *depend especially on the thoroughness with which you complete the first seven steps of Goal Development.*

FORM A PLANNING TASK FORCE

⬚**STEP 2:1**⬚ The first step is to form a "Planning Task Force."[1] The following checklist will guide you in selecting task force members.

Who, in our church, is best qualified to serve on a planning task force?

---

[1] If you already formed a "Planning Task Force" to carry out Phase I, proceed to ⬚Step 2:2⬚ .

CHECKLIST FOR SETTING UP A PLANNING TASK FORCE

1. Select persons who can accept an assignment and stay with it until it is completed. (If someone must drop out in the middle of the process, it will be extremely difficult for the replacement person to "get into" what is taking place.)
2. Select persons who are willing to attend a number of extra meetings during the next three to six months.
3. Select persons who, together, represent *all* your church's membership: the youth, the elderly, those with different lifestyles, etc. (If possible, more than one young person should be included in order to provide peer support.)
4. Select persons with positive feelings toward your church as well as persons who may be somewhat negative. *All* points of view should be represented.
5. Select persons who are willing to work through problems to reach some solution. (Compromise may be necessary for many task force decisions.)
6. Select persons who exhibit a strong commitment to Christ and His Church.

How can our pastor help to strengthen the planning process?

7. Select enough persons, but not too many. A task force should not have less than four or more than twelve persons, including the pastor. The following scale gives some suggested sizes:

If your church has:	Select as your task force:
up to 50 members	3 persons plus pastor
51 to 100 members	4 persons plus pastor
101 to 150 members	5 persons plus pastor
151 to 300 members	7 persons plus pastor
301 to 500 members	9 persons plus pastor
beyond 500 members	11 persons plus pastor

8. The individual you choose to serve as chairperson should have the administrative ability needed to help the task force to function effectively. The chairperson should be designated by the same group which appoints the task force.[2]

Once your task force has been appointed, you are ready to begin ⟦Step 2:2⟧ .

Note:
It is important that task force members come to know one another on a personal basis. Persons on the Planning Task Force will be working together for a number of months. Provide time for them to share their thinking with each other around the theme "What excites me about the church today is. . . ." Schedule at least one-half hour to do this in your first meeting. Also, ask the chairperson and/or your pastor to present a devotional based on one of the Scripture passages listed on page 26.

Using newsprint on the wall or a chartstand gets your ideas up so all can focus on them.

---

[2] It may be helpful to select co-chairpersons in larger situations; they can provide support for each other. Further, Planning Task Forces with more than eight persons may want to work in subgroups for many of the following steps. In this way all persons will have more opportunity to participate meaningfully.

LOOK AT YOUR PRESENT SITUATION

STEP 2:2

Two questions are basic here:
- What is your church currently doing?

and

- How do you feel about what your church is doing?

1. *WHAT IS YOUR CHURCH CURRENTLY DOING?*

Have on hand a supply of newsprint or other large-size paper. Put this on an easel or a wall, using masking tape. Ask someone from your group to serve as scribe at the newsprint. Provide a broad-tip felt marker so what is written is clearly visible to all.

Write on newsprint a list of what your church is presently doing. (Leave at least two inches between the items on the list. You will use this space later.) List services, ministries, programs—everything your Planning Task Force members can think of as "one of the things we do." Remember to include all activities through which your boards, committees, and organizations are doing the work of the church.

In addition, individual church members perform services and ministries at the church and in their homes and community. For instance: "Three teens sing in an ecumenical singing group." "Mary Smith conducts a Wednesday morning Bible study group in her home." "John Jones tutors children after school," etc. Be sure to include these.

You are probably doing more things than you realize; so the list will be long. At this stage, don't waste time debating unless something suggested *obviously* doesn't belong on the list.

What am I doing in this community?

2. HOW DO YOU FEEL ABOUT WHAT YOUR CHURCH IS DOING?

Human feelings are significant in every aspect of church and community life. Feelings both create and reveal the "climate" of a church. Each church has its own climate. Walk into a worship service and you can feel it. In some churches there is warmth, openness, excitement, while others seem rigid, cold, and dull.

Have you heard comments like these about your church or some other?

—I felt as if I were truly in the presence of God in church this morning.

—The singing is so slow I feel like falling asleep.

—I'm bored with church school.

—They made me feel as if they were glad I came.

In each case what is said is based on how the person feels about someone or something in the church.

Feelings are important. The feelings of your Planning Task Force members as well as those of your church family should be considered as you plan the future of your church. You are encouraged to use the Satisfaction Rating Scale described below. The results will give you some indication of what data should be gathered in ⏐Step 2:3⏐.

Satisfaction Rating Scale

Turn to what has been written on the newsprint. Put a letter before each item. Each member of your task force, working individually, should write on a piece of paper the letter identifying each item and a number from 1 to 10 to rate how he or she feels about *each* item. For instance, a "10" expresses satisfaction with the way the program or ministry is being done, while a "5" indicates a "so-so" feeling about it. A "1" indicates dissatisfaction with an item.

Illustration of the rating scale:

1	2	3	4	5	6	7	8	9	10
Dissatisfaction				Average "so-so"				Satisfaction	

As an example, you may rate an item with a 7, indicating that you feel more than "so-so" about it. To another you may give a 3, implying that better performance is needed.

Express your feelings honestly. Some of the things your church is doing may not rate very high. This is normal. You will have an opportunity later to consider what to do about items with low ratings.

NEWSPRINT LISTING	INDIVIDUAL WORKSHEET
a. Morning worship service	*a.* 9
b. Maintaining our building	*b.* 4
c. Senior high youth group	*c.* 2
d. Meals on Wheels	*d.* 8
e. Senior choir	*e.* 7
f. Evangelistic program	*f.* 3
Etc.	Etc.

Ask each person to go to the newsprint and under each item place the number he or she gave to it. *To arrive at a group score for each item,* total all the numbers and divide by the number of persons who participated. Write the result on the right side of the newsprint and draw a circle around it. Do this for each item.

THINGS WE ARE DOING . . . Av. Grade	
a. Morning worship service	
8, 7, 9, 8, 7, 3, 6, 9, 7	(7)
b. Maintaining our building	
9, 10, 10, 8, 7, 10, 8, 9, 9	(8.9)
c. Senior high youth group	
2, 3, 2, 1, 4, 4, 3, 3, 4	(2.9)
d. Meals on Wheels	
7, 9, 9, 10, 9, 8, 9, 9, 8	(8.7)
e. Senior choir	
1, 3, 4, 5, 2, 3, 3, 4, 5	(3.3)
f. Evangelistic program	
8, 7, 6, 9, 10, 8, 7, 6, 6	(7.4)
Etc.	

When you have finished this rating, the numbers placed after each item will give a general picture of how you feel about what your church is doing, the particular things you feel good about, and the things about which you feel less than satisfied.

Remember, this type of exercise indicates *only* how your Planning Task Force feels about the various things your church is doing. Interviewing some church members will help you check how well you represent the overall feelings of your congregation.

GATHER DATA ABOUT YOUR CHURCH, COMMUNITY, AND WORLD

STEP 2:3

To plan carefully, you need facts. Your church's ability to make responsible decisions about its future depends on how well the Planning Task Force secures accurate data about your church, its community, and the world.

Step 2:3 will take time and hard work. First efforts to collect facts always take more time than later efforts. In later planning it will be necessary only to update your existing data. Therefore, your Planning Task Force should invest now the time and energy required to collect the data recommended in this planning process.

Three kinds of data should be gathered to provide a base for making decisions:

1. Local church data
2. Community data
3. World data

Read through all the material for this step. On page 40 you will find instructions on how to gather the data described.

The forms and instruments needed to collect the three types of data for this planning process are listed below: [3]

1. *LOCAL CHURCH DATA*

To discover present and future church needs, you should be aware of membership characteristics.

a. Church and Church School Membership Table—Twenty Years
   —Membership line graph
   —Church School line graph

---

[3] In its appendix, LCPM contains instructions and tear-out work sheets required to gather the data described.

b. Membership Gain or Loss Table—Twenty Years
—Membership Methods bar graph

c. Church School Profile of current enrollment and average attendance
—Church School Profile graph

d. Money Received Table—Twenty Years
—Financial Support line graph

e. Contribution Table by Family Units
—Weekly Giving Profile graph

f. Distribution of the Church Dollar
—Circle graph

g. Church Participation Profile
—Church participation cards may be secured in quantity from National Ministries, American Baptist Churches in the U.S.A., Valley Forge, PA 19481.
—Tabulate participation profile summary and age-sex distribution
—Age-Sex Distribution bar graph

h. Church History Summary

i. Church Program Review
—Assign the task of writing reviews of church programs to each appropriate *unit* (or group) in your church. Follow the questions provided.

*j. Exploring Membership Attitudes: A Questionnaire Service[4]
—Questionnaire for Local Church Planning

*k. Role Expectations Checklist
—A selected list of items related to the total ministry of the church—to be responded to by the pastor and the laity to help determine the expectation levels of each other.

*l. Interviews
—Interviews can be conducted with both active and inactive members. It is as important to learn how inactive members feel about your church as it is to listen to active members.

2. *COMMUNITY DATA*
Define your community in terms of its limits created by nature

---

[4] Items with asterisks are optional.

and/or humans. Sometimes natural communities are easily recognized by local residents; at other times they are not. Within large cities, communities usually do not extend for more than a few square blocks, while in smaller cities they may encompass the entire city and some of the surrounding rural territory. In rural areas a community will quite frequently cover a township. In some sparsely settled areas the entire county will virtually be a community surrounding the county seat. Highways, means of travel, attitudes toward distance, and group identification are important in the community.

To define your community, consider the "effective service area" of your church. A basic question to ask is, "From what part of the area around our building can we reasonably expect to draw people to participate in our program?" Another basic question is, "How far does our influence extend?"

Gather data about the community you have defined as your effective service area. One of your best sources is the U.S. census.[5] Resources for gathering community data are:

a. Church Area and Neighborhood: Population Characteristics
   —Neighborhood Population Table
b. Employment Groups
c. Age-Sex Distribution, Area and Neighborhood Population
   —Age-Sex Distribution: Area bar graph
   —Age-Sex Distribution: Neighborhood bar graph
d. Housing in Church Neighborhood and Area
e. Community Interviews
   —Interviews provide your Planning Task Force with information not available in any other way.
f. Where Members and Constituents Live
   —Distance from Building bar graph
g. Maps
   —Family or Household Membership Map
   *—Evangelism Map[6]
   *—Church Location and Community Factors Map
*h. Where New Members Lived When They Joined

---

[5] The LCPM contains in its appendix resources for using Census materials and for conducting community interviews.
[6] Items with asterisks are optional.

3. WORLD DATA

International jet travel has convinced most of us that "it's a small, small world." Each church should be aware of how global issues and concerns affect it and how its ministry can influence them. We all have learned how a country on the other side of the world can raise oil prices and produce a chain of events that affect our families, our church's giving pattern, our church attendance, etc. Such direct links between "them" and "us" make us conscious that in the church we should be aware of global concerns and needs and what response we should make in light of the gospel.

Together, the churches of your denomination already have a worldwide perspective expressed through international missions. Such work must be continued. Now your church needs to expand its vision, examine all the needs on the world scene, and determine your response.

At this point make the following decisions:

First, establish a completion date for ⎡Step 2:3⎤.

Second, schedule some dates between now and then when your Planning Task Force can meet to report progress on its data gathering and to review this work. Ask members to protect these meeting dates in their personal calendars.

Third, after studying the options for ⎡Step 2:3⎤, determine how much time and energy you can invest in collecting the data necessary to make good decisions.

Your Planning Task Force must make the final decision about which and how much data should be gathered. The more thorough your data gathering, the more successful your planning will be.

Fourth, decide which of the forms and instruments described on pages 38-40 you will use. Check to see if any task force members have special interests or preferences in working with certain forms. Divide the work so all members are involved, either individually or in small groups. Make sure each type of data you have decided to gather is assigned to an individual or group. Enlist other resource persons in your church to help you (e.g., ask your church clerk to get twenty-year attendance and membership figures; ask the church school secretary for church school statistics, etc.). World data might be handled best by your Planning Task Force working as a total group.

PREPARE AN INFORMATION SUMMARY

STEP 2:4

In the previous two steps of Goal Development, your Planning Task Force identified and evaluated current church programs and ministries, and collected data about your church, its community, and the world. You should now create an "Information Summary" from the facts and opinions you have gathered.

Prepare your Information Summary by acting on your answers to the following two questions:

- Who on your Planning Task Force should organize the data?
  1. You could do this work as a committee of the whole.
  2. Two or three of your members with a particular interest in this step could volunteer.
  3. Your chairperson could appoint a subcommittee. (A minimum of three persons should serve, regardless of the size of your task force.)

The amount of data gathered may require several work sessions to get it ready for the Planning Task Force meeting at which it will be used.

- What is the best way to organize the data? (Use one of the following options or create one of your own.)

  Option 1—*Place under each of the following categories the information related to it.*[7]

  a. Developing spiritually vital church members.

  b. Expanding educational ministries.

  c. Performing Christ's work in the community.

  d. Sharing Christ with unbelievers.

  e. Extending our mission throughout the world.

  f. Making our church life more productive and efficient through improved operations.

  All statistics, interview answers, program evaluations, and other material that belong to one of the six categories should be pulled together into one block of information. Some data may relate to more than one category; put these data under *each* category to which they relate.

  Option 2—*Sort the material according to its own general type, something like this:*

---

[7] Note: This book and LCPM follow Option 1 for their examples and illustrations.

a. *Statistical data:* counts taken on church membership, youth activities, records of church finances, the community age-sex profile, housing starts, changes in community population, etc.

b. *Program reviews and evaluations:* information from boards and committees related to your church's program.

c. *Interviews:* opinions expressed by program leaders, community leaders, etc.

d. *Self-study findings:* Task Force findings from
Step 2:2 covering: what you are doing, and how you feel about what you are doing; other findings: church participation survey, questionnaire for local church planning, role-expectation checklist, etc.

Before you begin either of these two options, set a date for the Planning Task Force meeting at which you will begin work on Step 2:5 or Step 2:6. This date will become the target for your information organizers to complete their work.

Now, begin work on your Information Summary.

STEP 2:5 (An optional step carried on pages 36-38 of LCPM.)

LIST YOUR ASSUMPTIONS: *What Do You Believe About Your God, Your Church, Your World?*

STEP 2:6 Refer to the work you have done in earlier steps to help you spell out what you believe:

• about the task to which God is calling you as a congregation (See your Statement of Purpose.)

• about the environment in which you will minister to answer the call (See your Information Summary.)

• about how your church does/will operate to do its mission (See your final list from Step 2:5.)

WHAT IS AN ASSUMPTION?

An *assumption* . . .

—is what you believe to be true and are willing to act upon.

—makes you confident even when you lack complete information.

—is your judgment of what the available facts mean.

—is the foundation upon which your church's goals, objectives, and program plans rest.

It is important to examine what you assume or believe to be true before you begin to write any goals for your church. A belief can be expressed as one of three kinds of assumptions: theological, environmental or operational.

It is important that all members of your task force understand the term "assumption."

AN EVERYDAY-LIFE ILLUSTRATION

Everyday life is based on assumptions. We don't always check each one because that would take too much time; however, when we wrongly assume something, trouble can start! Here is a personal illustration:

One winter my 2½-year-old son accompanied me on some afternoon pastoral calls. I don't like to struggle with little boys' boots, so I had been carrying him through the snow between each house and the car. When we came home from the visits, I carried him to the porch of the parsonage and placed him on his feet at the door. The winter wind was near gale force. When I finally got the door open, I expected him to go in, but all he did was lean forward. I suggested, in competition with the howling wind, that we ought to go in, to which the only response was an inquiring look and a little more leaning.

Shouting over the wind, I suggested to him that if he didn't move, I was going to help him by placing a hand "he knew where." Still fighting the wind and the door (while heating the out-of-doors), I raised my hand to offer some persuasion at the proper place, and in so doing saw something. One of his shoestrings was untied, and I was standing on it! He couldn't have moved even if he had wanted to!

When I checked my assumptions, I discovered a fact that changed the whole situation. (Can you spot my wrong assumption?)[8]

---

[8] I had assumed he had full control over both feet.

Clarifying basic assumptions early can avoid many conflicts down the road.

1. CLARIFY YOUR ASSUMPTIONS

Each church member has a set of assumptions. At times church members may have different assumptions about the same thing. It is important to provide opportunities to discuss these differences to bring about better understanding. As you can imagine, even mild disagreements on basic assumptions, if not recognized and taken into account, can mean trouble for your church.

Assumptions can express our beliefs both about how things are presently and about how things will be in the future. For instance, considering what you know now, what do you think your neighborhood will be like five years from now? Do you expect things to remain as they are? Or do you anticipate changes that will require corresponding change in the mission of your church? What world developments do you expect will call for a change in your church's thrust and style of mission?

Today a church must be active, flexible, and competitive to have a vital influence within the world it is called to serve. In the midst of rapid social and environmental changes, no church can deal well with today's problems by using yesterday's assumptions—as if change was not taking place. To do so condemns any church's future to be simply a faster repetition of its past.

We, of course, cannot be *certain* about the future. However, to avoid repeating automatically in the future what your church has been doing, you should from time to time update or reaffirm your assumptions; the *theological,* the *environmental,* and the *operational.*

2. STUDY SOME EXAMPLES

Example: Loyal (and well-meaning) Christian education leaders in the local church often deal again and again with plans for Rally

Day, a Christmas party, a summer picnic, and Easter egg hunts. Such leaders seldom find the time to discuss crucial issues, such as the quality of church school teaching, the nature of student interest, or the kind of support system needed by those who teach. Those who look only at Rally Days, special parties, etc., probably work from some of the following assumptions:

—We will always have a church school.

—Our congregation expects special seasonal programs.

—Anyone we recruit to teach is capable of doing the job.

—Even though our community is changing, the difference will not require changes in what we offer through our church school.

—Most of our "kids" will not drop out of church school.

—God expects special programs in church school.

—All church schools have declining attendance; so our decline is normal.

Example: Diaconate boards often think of themselves as evangelistic, the spiritual leaders in their church. Yet many boards appear to operate on such assumptions as:

—If we keep our church open, God will give an increase.

—It's the pastor's job to win people; we pay the pastor to do this kind of work.

—Our attendance will stay about where it is, no matter what we do.

—We should put our own house in order before going outside our congregation to reach others.

—If we only had some training, we could share our faith, but we haven't; so . . .

—People today really aren't interested in either the gospel or the local church.

Note that in these examples all three types of assumptions were included: *theological, environmental,* and *operational.*

3. *WRITE YOUR THEOLOGICAL ASSUMPTIONS*[9]

Theological assumptions are statements about what you believe

---

[9] An option in large churches is to divide the task force into three groups and to work on the three categories of assumptions at the same time.

God *because of God's nature* is calling the people of God to do *because of their nature.* Valid theological assumptions are your deepest feelings able to be acted upon. In other words, theological assumptions relate to how you intend to act. Some discussion-starter questions are: What do *you* believe about God? On what do *you* base *your* religious beliefs? What do *you* believe about Jesus Christ? What do *you* believe about the Bible that causes you to take certain actions? What is the role of prayer in *your* life? Here are some examples of theological assumptions:

a. God exists.

b. God creates.

c. God cares for all creation.

d. Jesus Christ, God's Son, died for our sins to establish fellowship between us and God.

e. The Church expresses God's love and forgiveness and is the symbol and sign that God has brought hope and healing to persons through Jesus Christ.

f. The Bible is the authority for what we believe.

g. The Holy Spirit witnesses to our spirits within and beyond the Scriptures.

h. God wants us to be involved in the world's healing.

i. Attending church regularly strengthens persons spiritually. (Worship puts power in persons' lives.)

j. God has a job for our church to do where we are right now.

k. The love of God, revealed in Jesus Christ, is for all persons who confess their sins and ask forgiveness.

l. The Holy Spirit gives power to any who seek to do God's will.

List your theological assumption statements on newsprint. Save for future reference.

4. WRITE YOUR ENVIRONMENTAL ASSUMPTIONS

Environmental Assumptions are what you believe to be true about your *community and the world,* the *contexts in which you live.* Environmental assumptions should describe your town or city, county, and state, as well as the worldwide situations that could both affect and be affected by your congregation. Here are some environmental assumptions:

a. The average wage level in our area will go up (two new industries are moving in, and our closed coal mines will be reopened soon).
b. There will be a shorter work week within the next five years.
c. Within the next decade, the neighborhood immediately surrounding our church will *not* be an ideal place for families with young children.
d. _____ percent of the residents in our immediate community will be retired by 19_____.
e. A year-round schedule will soon be used in our public schools.
f. More families will require some kind of day-care assistance for young children by 19_____.
g. Within five years, changing family patterns will force us to create new educational patterns and settings or go out of the business of Christian education.
h. By 19_____, there will be _____ percent more retirees and older adults in our community with empty time on their hands.

List your environmental assumptions on newsprint. Save for future reference.

5. *WRITE YOUR OPERATIONAL ASSUMPTIONS*

Operational Assumptions are what you believe to be true about your church's *traditions, organization,* and *ways of operating* (how it goes about doing its work). What do you believe is true now and/or will be true in the future about your facilities, professional and lay leadership, budget, the methods you use to organize your church to carry out its ministries? Some examples are:

a. Our church will grow spiritually and numerically.
b. Our church will possess an increased sense of responsibility for ministry in its neighborhood.
c. Our next pastor will receive a housing allowance to buy his or her own home.
d. Our budget will double in the next six years.
e. Our congregation will fall apart because of an increasing unwillingness of lay persons to accept designated leadership positions.
f. Our church will be in a new building program by 19_____.
g. Five years from now, by maintaining our present rate of

growth, we will need additional professional staff.

h. Five years from now we will have enough money to support both a full-time pastor and a full-time associate pastor.

i. By 19___, ___ percent of our membership under fifty years of age will live more than three miles from our church building.

j. A day-care center will be started by our church.

k. We will have more types of family programs by 19___.

l. In the next decade our major membership growth will come through receiving members from neighborhood minority groups.

List your operational assumptions on newsprint. Save for future reference.

6. *FURTHER INSTRUCTIONS*

Make arrangements to share your assumptions with each of the church's boards and committees. Make copies of the lists. Ask each Planning Task Force member to do two things: (1) give a copy to every member of the board(s) or committee(s) for which he or she acts as the contact; (2) meet with the board or committee to review and expand the assumption lists and to find out its level of agreement with each assumption. Point out that assumptions become the base from which to write goals. Take all responses back to your Planning Task Force for summarizing and study.

Publish the summarized assumptions in your church newsletter or other media. Explain them to your total membership. Ask all members to make suggestions about the list. Ask church classes, small groups, and other organizations to discuss the assumptions.

IDENTIFY NEEDS AND CONCERNS

| STEP 2:7 | When you have completed Step 2:6, both your Information Summary and your listing of assumptions will be available to the Planning Task Force as it begins |

one of the most significant steps in planning—writing your church's goals. The chairperson and the pastor should prepare for Step 2:7 by selecting appropriate Scriptures which can help define areas of concern. For instance, what were some concerns of Jesus and what caused these concerns as illustrated in the verse "Jesus wept" (John 11:35)?

Begin │Step 2:7│ by asking, "What do our assumption lists say about us as a church?" How you go about fulfilling your purpose will depend on how you see the needs of your members, your community, and the world. Review your assumptions to identify your congregation's major areas of concern.

An *Area of Concern* is something about your church life, your community, or the world that calls your congregation to act because of the way your church has stated its purpose and assumptions. Now that you have summarized your data (your Information Summary) and prepared your assumptions in light of them, begin to look within the data for indications of:

- Issues
- Problems
- Opportunities/Challenges
- Needs

Each of these four items can be a signpost directing you to an area of concern:

Issues—An issue is a situation in the life of your church or community about which persons have taken positions, for or against. Issues may involve personal relationships, social circumstances, finances, or other tensions. It takes courage to raise sensitive issues.

Problems—A problem is a condition demanding solution. Problems, whether in the church, the community, or both, cannot be ignored when doing long-range planning. Planning in your church depends on your refusal to ignore problems and your willingness to work at solving them!

Opportunities/Challenges—Some circumstances remain largely untreated until the *church* takes the initiative to respond. The very nature of such circumstances invites church involvement (for example, sponsoring refugees). We call these circumstances "opportunities," or sometimes, "challenges."

Needs—Needs are situations requiring relief. Needs can touch individuals, families, groups, organizations, and the environment. Needs are both local and worldwide. Institutions often find renewed vitality by searching for and responding to real needs.

A *problem* may represent someone's *need* which, at the same time, can be an *opportunity* or *challenge* for your church's ministry. Items from your Information Summary or assumption lists define an Area of Concern.

In a diagram, it might look like this:

An Issue — — — — — — — — — —
A Problem — — — — — — — — — → AN AREA OF CONCERN
An Opportunity/Challenge — — — — — — — —
A Need — — — —

A Worship Example

Suppose your purpose statement says, "God invites us to experience a personal, worshipful relationship with Him." Suppose your Task Force has discovered from its data gathering that a substantial number of persons (members and neighbors) do not worship regularly because they "don't get any sense of the presence of God" from your worship services. If one of your assumptions says, "Our church meets the worship needs of its members and its community," obviously there is a *problem* to be faced. It should be listed on your newsprint as a major *area of concern* requiring attention.

Suppose, further, another of your assumptions states, "The best hour for worship is at 11:00 A.M. on Sunday morning." Your Information Summary says that some of your members are infirm and do not leave home for any reason. The summary also shows that a number of church families spend weekends at recreation centers. If your data are true, you will have been acting on incorrect assumptions. This is a good reason why worship should be considered an *area of concern* by the congregation.

A Fellowship Example

Now suppose your church purpose statement says, "God wants us to live together in fellowship as His family." From your Information Summary you know that several church members (and even more persons in the church's neighborhood) go for months without any meaningful visits or fellowship. You also find your church has not provided small groups where individuals or couples can get together on their own for prayer and Bible study, for social hours after services, for work projects, or for special events. Yet, one of your theological assumptions says, "God calls us to love one another." You have identified an obvious *problem* which is also a *challenge and an opportunity;* list it as a major *area of concern.*

A Mission Example

Suppose, further, that your purpose statement says, "Our Lord, Jesus Christ, has charged us to go into the world to preach, to teach, to heal, and to help." But your Information Summary tells you few members know what your church is doing in evangelism and social action; in fact, they know so little they cannot say whether they agree or disagree with it. Two of your theological assumptions state, "Jesus Christ, God's Son, died for our sins to establish fellowship between us and God," and, "God wants us to be involved in the world's healing." Note the tension between these theological assumptions and the Information Summary. The *issue* of your congregation's lack of mission awareness should be listed as a major *area of concern* for your Planning Task Force.

An Education Example

Further, your Information Summary shows many members say they do not know what they believe well enough to share their faith with others. One of your operational assumptions states: "Our current church school program fails to prepare our members for mission." An education and training *problem* should be added to your list as an *area of concern*.

The four examples given above suggest a style for identifying and defining your Areas of Concern. Other concerns will emerge as you study your assumption lists and Information Summary. In Step 2:8 your task will be to write goals which guide you in responding to these concerns.

Now if back on page 42 you elected to use Option #1 for your reporting style, your Areas of Concern can be placed in the categories recommended by this planning process. If you elected to use Option #2 or some other reporting style, you will need to create your own categories for your Areas of Concern. Your categories can then be compared with the examples shown in this book (or in the more complete illustrations given in LCPM).

To review, **Option #1** categories are:
A. Developing spiritually vital church members.
B. Expanding educational ministries.
C. Performing Christ's work in the community.
D. Sharing Christ with unbelievers.
E. Extending our mission throughout the world.
F. Making our church life more productive and efficient through improved operations.

Put six sheets of newsprint on the wall. At the top of each sheet write one of the above six categories, A through F, or use your own categories. Draw a vertical line down the middle of each newsprint sheet. To the left of the line write the issues, problems, opportunities/challenges, or needs you have identified. To the right of the line, list the related Area(s) of Concern you have identified.

Illustration:

A. DEVELOPING SPIRITUALLY VITAL CHURCH MEMBERS	
INFORMATION Church attendance is down Many members are inactive Lack of enthusiasm A few people are doing all the work Difficulty raising budget	**CONCERN** Inactive church members

Some examples are given below to show how Areas of Concern can be fitted into one or another of the six categories A through F. Only one piece of information and one related concern are listed for each example. Your actual list will probably include many pieces of information and a number of concerns related to each category.
EXAMPLES:

Category A. Developing spiritually vital church members.
—*Information:* Many of our church members are inactive. (This could identify a problem, define a need or an opportunity.)
—*Concern:* Inactive church members

53

Category B.   Expanding educational ministries.
—*Information:*   Church school attendance is down 8 percent from last year.
—*Concern:*   Decline in church school attendance.

Category C.   Performing Christ's Work in the community.
—*Information:*   None of our members serve on a community board or committee.
—*Concern:*   Lack of Christian influence in community affairs.

Category D.   Sharing Christ with unbelievers.
—*Information:*   Few of our church members are witnessing Christians.
—*Concern:*   Lack of witnessing Christians.

Category E.   Extending our mission throughout the world.
—*Information:*   World hunger is increasing.
—*Concern:*   Thousands of persons around the world are starving.

Category F.   Making our church life more productive and efficient through improved operations.
—*Information:*   Our old furnace is using more fuel than two years ago.
—*Concern:*   It costs too much to heat our building.

Look for an order of priority emerging among the Areas of Concern you have listed. Identify the Areas you feel should receive immediate attention.

Place a "1" next to those Areas of Concern you feel need top priority attention. Do not limit yourself necessarily to one "1"; perhaps several of your concerns will require quick attention. Then, place a "2," "3," "4," etc., after each remaining item to indicate what you feel is its level of urgency.

If more than one Area of Concern receives a "1" priority, consider each of these concerns until you have been able to choose what you feel is the *number one Area of Concern for your church* and have placed the others in priority order beneath it. Use fresh newsprint to copy your Areas of Concern in priority order.

Getting Ready for Step 2:8

The Planning Task Force chairperson should, before the next meeting, make arrangements to have available the materials and resources necessary for writing goal statements. These would include your *Areas of Concern* in priority order, your *assumption* lists, your *Information Summary,* and the *Purpose Statement* of your church.

Have an ample supply of newsprint available for Step 2:8 .

Both the Old and New Testaments provide many illustrations of goals. Begin your session on Step 2:8 with a devotional centered on one of these. Ask God's guidance as you work on your goals.

Stating Goals

Planning is based on a continuous movement from purpose to goals.

PURPOSE→ GOALS

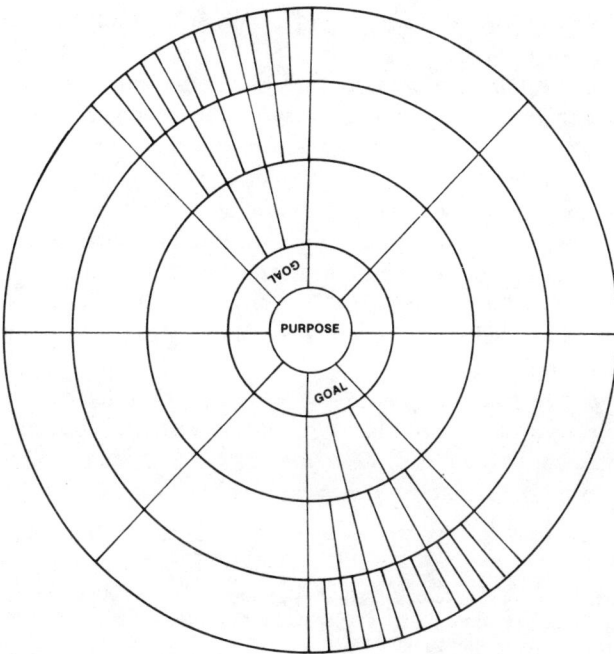

WRITE GOALS

STEP 2:8

A goal expresses *a condition or "end-state" you wish to attain.*[10] It should be rooted in the purpose of your congregation and should always reflect your Purpose Statement.

The goals you prepare should be easily understood by your members and should express their desired long-range results of ministry.

Each goal should focus on what your major accomplishments in mission ought to be in light of your Purpose Statement. Church goals must be "owned" if they are, in fact, to gain your congregation's attention and focus its resources (its time, personnel, finances, and facilities).

Goal statements, when correctly written, do not mention program details or any "how to" steps. Means and methods for pursuing goals are dealt with later in the planning process.

Some aids for writing vital goal statements:

1. *Be clear in what you say.* Avoid jargon or unfamiliar theological words or phrases.
2. *Have one point (or focus) for each goal statement.* If your goal has more than one main point, use more than one goal statement.
3. *Be sure your goal statement says only what the final result (end-state) will be, not how you will reach it.* Do not include what you will do to achieve your goal. Program plans, time frames, program costs, who will perform certain tasks, etc., are dealt with later.
4. *Be concise.* State *briefly* what the end-state or condition will be.
5. *Make the goal statement challenging and realistic,* neither so easy that people will not be motivated, nor so gigantic as to produce frustration.
6. *Goal statements should reflect your purpose statement.* In other words, you should be able to point to a concept in your purpose statement that calls for each goal.
7. Keep in mind that *your members will need to "buy in" to each goal.* You will need their support if it is to be accomplished.

---

[10] Perhaps the most misused term in the planning process is the word "goal." Many persons confuse program plans or objectives with goals. See the definitions of these terms in the front of the book.

AN EXERCISE

To test your understanding of what the goal should be, read the following illustration and try your hand at writing a goal statement related to it.

Suppose on a warm and sunny day you arrive at the shore of a beautiful lake. You hear that across the lake, beyond reach by car, is a scenic waterfall. To see this sight, one must go to the other side of the lake. You decide to see the waterfall. After making some inquiries, you discover there are rowboats, canoes, and motorboats for rent. Upon further checking, you find that an excursion boat crosses the lake at frequent intervals. Besides all these possibilities, you are a good swimmer and happen to have your bathing suit along!

What would be your goal in this situation? Read the story again if necessary. Write your goal statement below:

Now check what you have written. Does your statement contain anything about your need to get to the other side of the lake? Does it say anything about the means of transportation for crossing the lake? It shouldn't.

The goal from this short story is simply, "To view the waterfall." Such a goal is short, concise, and to the point.

It might appear, at first, that your goal would be to get to the other side of the lake. Getting to the other side, however, as well as the way used to get there are means (program plans)[11] employed *in order to view the waterfall.* The goal statement itself should include nothing about means (how you are going to get there, how much it will cost, how much time it will take, etc.). The goal statement should indicate only the end result you seek.

---

[11] Remember, program plans are treated later in this planning process.

TYPES OF GOAL STATEMENTS

Goal statements fit either of two types: *one type* covers goals which reflect the church's total mission, goals common to everyone in the congregation; *the other type* covers goals pointing to a particular group, age level, or area of interest. A total mission goal might reflect the intentions of all members of your congregation about the Sunday morning worship service. A particular goal might deal with the needs of your church's youth in the morning worship service.

WHO SHOULD PARTICIPATE IN WRITING GOALS

It is helpful and proper to involve persons beyond the Planning Task Force in goal writing, especially persons who will be directly affected. Some benefits of involving others are:

1. It broadens participation in your planning process.
2. More persons will know that goal statements are being developed.
3. It can provide additional ideas and, perhaps, resources.
4. There will be greater understanding of what the goal statements mean.
5. More persons will tend to "own" the goals created in this fashion.

Involve as many people as possible in creating the church's goal statements.

This planning process offers three options for involving others in writing goals (and objectives).[12] The basic concept is that your *Planning Task Force cannot and should not, on its own, try to write the congregation's goals* and then expect church members to "buy in" and support them. Try to involve others in writing goal statements *at the level of their interest or responsibility.* Your pastor should be invited to each goal-writing session. You may also want to invite your area minister or another consultant to work with you as you write your goals.

Option #1

Many churches have committees, task forces, or boards whose work fits within the categories listed on page 53. If your church is organized in this way, then you already have a list of leaders whom you should involve in writing goal statements. For example:

Category A: *Developing spiritually vital church members.*
Church council
Diaconate
Nurture commission
Spiritual committee
Worship committee

Category B: *Expanding educational ministries.*
Representatives of each age level
Board or commission of Christan education
Church school superintendent
Education specialists or volunteers

Category C: *Performing Christ's work in the community.*
Age level organizations
Diaconate
Outreach committee
Small-group representatives
Social concerns committee

---

[12] Whether you choose Option #1 or Option #2, a further choice is to begin writing *objectives* during the same session at which you are working on *goal statements.* This can be done if you handle only one or two Areas of Concern at each of your goal-writing sessions and use only a little time to write the goal statements. If you choose to work on goals and objectives at the same time, read and study ⌐Step 2:9⌐ (Write Objectives) well ahead of time to make the best use of the hours your goal-writing group(s) is/are together.

Category D: *Sharing Christ with unbelievers.*
Diaconate
Evangelism committee
Outreach committee
Witness commission
Category E: *Extending our mission throughout the world.*
Committee or board of missions
School of missions chairperson
Small groups (women's organization, etc.)
Category F: *Making our church life more productive and efficient through improved operations.*
Board of trustees
Pastoral relations committee
Personnel committee

When many are involved in goal writing, a number of sessions will probably be needed to get the job done. Get one or more representatives from each group in advance of your scheduled goal-writing sessions to ensure maximum participation.

Option #2

The membership of your Planning Task Force may include representatives from all church boards and committees. These persons can serve as communicators between the groups they represent and the Planning Task Force. In this option the Planning Task Force studies its Areas of Concerns and defines possible goals. This work can then be communicated to each board or committee. Each board or committee, in turn, will study the task force's work, possibly revise it, and send it back. Once the Planning Task Force receives the full review and is satisfied with the revisions, it can return the goal statement(s) to the committees and boards for a final check before they are given to the congregation (or official board) for study and action.

Option #3

Another option would be for the Planning Task Force to share with each board or committee the Areas of Concern (and related background material) from ⬚ Step 2:7 ⬚ . Each group would be asked to analyze the material and suggest possible goals. The results could then come to the Planning Task Force for refinement. After this, the refined goal statements would be returned to each board or committee for a final review before being given to the congregation.

GETTING PERSONS READY TO WRITE GOAL STATEMENTS

Any persons who join you to write goals should be given the background materials the Planning Task Force chairperson gathered according to the instructions on page 55. Take time to acquaint them with what was done in ⬚ Step 2:7 ⬚ . Don't rush through this important orientation. Help them understand what led you to identify each Area of Concern. This is important since *each* goal should reflect a *major* Area of Concern you have identified. Each Area of Concern implies one goal. Display the newsprint from ⬚ Step 2:7 ⬚ on which you listed your concerns in priority order.

WRITING YOUR GOAL STATEMENTS

By this point, you should have: (1) studied the definitions and the principles about goal statements; (2) used the exercise on page 57; (3) decided which option to follow to involve others; (4) prepared other persons to work with you. Now, write your goal statements by taking each Area of Concern in priority order.

As you write, don't hesitate to strike out words or phrases or add suggestions made by the group. Write a goal all over again when necessary. When the writing group has agreed on a goal statement, write it on a clean sheet of newsprint and move on to another Area of Concern.

An Example

Here is an example of a goal statement for Category A used to illustrate the mission of your church.

Category A: *Developing spiritually vital church members.*
Area of Concern: Inactive church members

61

Goal: A majority of our church members will be
active in the mission of our church.
Illustration:

A. Developing Spiritually Vital Church Members	
Concern Inactive church members	**Goal** A majority of our members will be active in the mission of our church.

TEST YOUR GOAL STATEMENTS
Ask five questions about each of your goal statements:
1. *Does the goal statement say anything?*
   If it does, does it speak clearly? Some goal statements sound
   very impressive and attractive but mean something different to
   each reader. Does your statement mean about the same thing to
   each person who reads it?
2. *Is the goal attainable by your church?*
   If the goal, as stated, is obviously impossible for your church
   group to accomplish, revise the statement until your members
   feel they can make reasonable progress toward it.
3. *Does the goal reflect the Purpose Statement of your church?*
   Be able to identify which part of your Purpose Statement relates
   to each goal.
4. *Will your membership "own" the goal?*
   "Ownership" by your members is imperative. Will your
   congregation work to achieve this goal?
5. *Does the goal statement point only to one desired end-state?*
   Be sure the goal statement has only one focus and does not say
   anything about how you will reach the end-state.
Then, ask one more question.
*How completely do your goal statements, when considered together,
cover what is implied by your statement of purpose?*

Check to see what areas of your Purpose Statement are not touched by the goals you have defined. If there are some untouched areas, keep writing.

Setting Objectives

Planning is based on a continuous movement from purpose to goals; from goals to their related objectives.

Purpose————➤Goals————➤Objectives

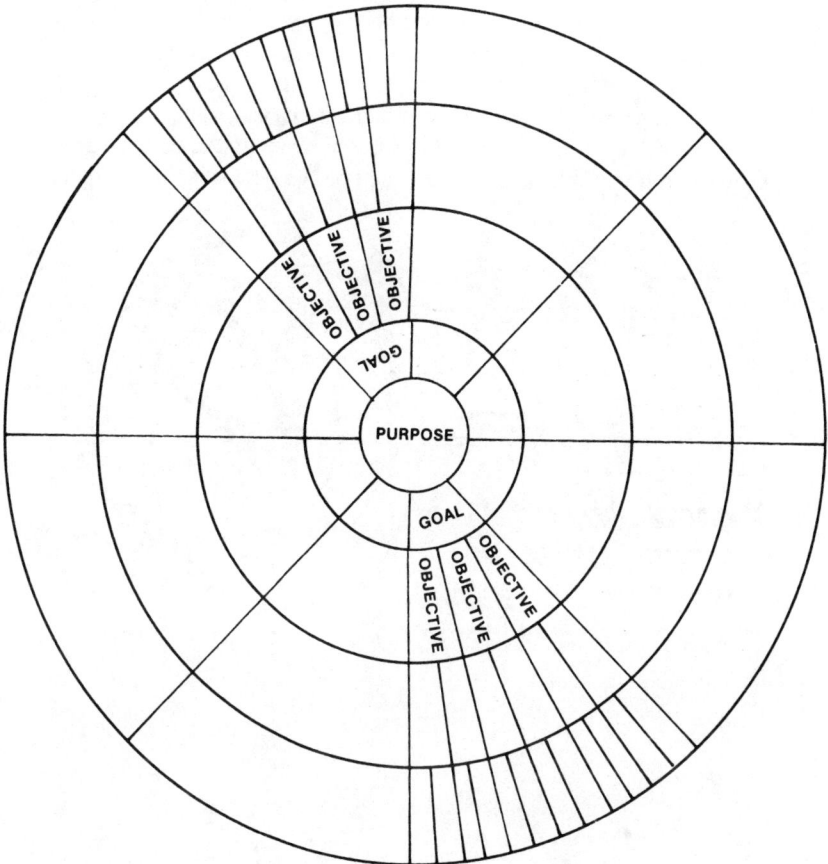

WRITE OBJECTIVES

STEP
2:9

An objective is *a clear, simple statement of a target to be reached.* It is derived from a goal statement. Usually you will be able to identify several objectives for each goal. (See the above diagram.) As an example, one group wrote sixteen objectives for the same goal. Each of the sixteen expressed a distinct part of that goal.

Objectives can be classified by the time period needed to achieve them. *Short-term* objectives imply time periods of two years or less; *long-term* objectives refer to time periods of more than two years. Many planners feel that five-year time blocks set a good range for long-term objectives. Except in unusual circumstances, program planners seldom try to project beyond a five- to ten-year period.

An objective should be stated so its achievement can be measured, in order to test movement toward the goal to which it is related. To

A good objective statement is a target to be reached. It has an action verb.

determine if the objective can be measured, answer such questions as these:

—Who, or what persons, are to be involved or helped?

—How many? How much?

—Where?

—When? (Beginning when? Accomplished when?)

A good objective statement has one verb implying a specific action, such as *write, interview, organize, invite, vote, build, tutor, design,* etc. Avoid vague or general action verbs, such as *understand, serve, grow,* etc.[13]

A sample objectives worksheet, using Category A and its goal identified earlier on pages 61-62, is given below as the worksheet might be written on newsprint.

OBJECTIVES WORKSHEET
Category A: Developing spiritually vital church members
Area of Concern: Inactive church members
Goal: A majority of our members will be active in the mission of our church.
Objectives: —Within two months, our congregation will officially adopt a common definition for the terms "active members" and "inactive members." ST* —Within two months after our congregation adopts the definitions, each church member will be placed on either an active member or inactive member list. ST* —Within three months, our congregation will approve at least two new plans to involve our inactive members in the life and ministry of our church. ST* —Within three years from the time we begin to carry out the new plans to involve inactive members, we will have 30 percent of them involved in our church mission. LT**

*Short Term
**Long Term

---

[13] Appendix J of LCPM illustrates five principles to follow in choosing action verbs for objectives.

Comment: Obviously, several more objectives could be written for this goal statement. Do not limit your thinking to three or four objectives for each goal. Include as many objectives as you can. Later you will decide which objectives best fit your church. Meanwhile, "the sky's the limit."

Begin writing objectives by selecting the goal statement related to the Area of Concern chosen as "number one" by your church group. Describe some specifics that will help to achieve a part of what the goal states. Be careful *not* to include in objective statements any "how to" (the methods or program plans that might be used to reach the objective).

Study your goal statements and write down all related objectives that occur to you. Do not limit yourself. Later in the planning process there will be time for comparing the objectives to choose which ones your church will use. Use newsprint and follow the style you used to develop your goal statements. (See page 65.)

GETTING YOUR OBJECTIVES READY FOR USE IN EVALUATION

You read on page 64 that an objective is derived from a goal statement (a desired long-range result of ministry). You also read that an objective should be written so you can measure its achievement. These ideas point to the reasons for objectives. Planners write objectives in order to divide a goal into pieces which: (1) can be handled within a reasonable time period (ranging from a few weeks to two years or so) and (2) can be handled so you know what is being accomplished. Well-stated objectives, then, have at least two specific uses:

1. A well-stated objective sharpens the focus for *action*. It increases the possibility of developing program plans and program plan details (see Phase III) that will work in your church's situation.
2. A well-stated objective sharpens the focus for *reflection*. It helps you to decide how well your program plan moved toward what was intended and how you can improve future program plans.

Reflection involves "evaluation." In this planning process evaluation is dealt with fully in Phase V. However, it is important here to introduce a few evaluation ideas:

- An objective states what a planner intends or expects to result from what is done.
- Evaluation involves deciding how well you accomplished what was expected or intended when you wrote your objective.
- Such expectations or intentions imply *clues* or *signs,* called criteria.
- A good objective statement will point to its criteria—what the planner should look for, observe, count, or measure in some way as a basis for evaluation.

The *criteria* implied by a stated objective (that is, the clues or signs) are evidence which provide a way of checking how much of the objective has been achieved and how well the program plan helped in the achievement.

Defining criteria for each objective points to things which two or more observers can see, taste, touch, smell, hear, or at least be aware of in some conscious way. As always, "beauty is in the eye of the beholder." However, by setting criteria, you make it possible for two or more persons to agree on the clues or signs of "beauty" and on how much "beauty" is present in a given instance.

The marks of good clues or signs (criteria) are:
1. Each must be valid—that is, it must be a faithful measure for that objective.
2. Each must be reliable—that is, it must measure similar things in the same way each time it is used.
3. Each must be reasonable in cost—that is, it must not be too expensive to use (to observe and to record).
4, Each must be legitimate—that is, it must respect the individual's right for privacy.

At this point take each objective as you have stated it and decide what measurable criteria (clues or signs) you will use. Include these criteria in an indented paragraph under each of your stated objectives.

We illustrate some criteria by using the first objective developed in Category A.

OBJECTIVES WORKSHEET

Category A: Developing spiritually vital church members

Area of Concern: Inactive church members

Goal: A majority of our members will be active in the mission of our church.

Objective: —Within two months, our congregation will officially adopt a common definition for the terms "active members" and "inactive members."   ST

Criteria:
- One church group has carried full responsibility for developing the definitions and bringing these to the congregation for action.
- The objective was achieved within the eight-week period set for it.
- The members of the congregation, before voting on the definitions, had at least two opportunities, as required by our bylaws, to become familiar with the definitions and how they would be used.
- The minutes of church board, committee, commission meetings show that the definitions were discussed in such elected bodies before the congregation was asked to vote.
- The official minutes of the church carry a record of the congregation's favorable vote on the definitions and their use.

Objective: —Within two months after our congregation adopts the definitions, each church member will be placed on either an active member or inactive member list.   ST

Criteria:

SET PRIORITIES AMONG OBJECTIVES

| STEP 2:10 |

Begin this step with a Bible study. Read 1 Peter 2:9-21. Discuss what it means to be God's own people. Close your Bible study with prayer asking God's help in setting priorities among your objectives.

From Step 2:7 your goal statements are in order according to the priorities you set among your Areas of Concern.

If you are like most Planning Task Forces, you have probably written more objectives for each goal than your congregation can work on at one time. Use the guidelines given below to examine each objectives worksheet. Mark each objective with the number of each guideline that applies. For example, objectives which fit the foundation guideline should be marked with a "2."

GUIDELINES FOR PUTTING OBJECTIVES INTO PRIORITY ORDER

1. *Objectives Based on What the Bible Is Saying to Your Congregation*

    In ⎡Step 2:6⎤ you listed your church's biblical and theological assumptions. Study that list again. What should your church be doing in light of your biblical and theological assumptions?

What does the Bible say to us about priorities?

    Does the way you have declared the mission of your church require that certain functions be carried out, e.g., evangelism, ministry to others, etc.?

2. *Foundation Objectives*

    The statement "We must achieve this objective if we are to be in a position to minister to others" illustrates foundation objectives. "To have a pastor, we must pay a living salary." "To use a church building, we must maintain it." Not to achieve foundation objectives means you simply can't continue to serve as an organized congregation.

3. *What's Near Your Church Doorstep?*

    Certain special needs may exist in the community immediately surrounding your church property. What can you do to respond to them? What are the opportunities for service God has put on your doorstep?

4. *Ready Resources*

Can the objective be met rather easily because the congregation already has available to it special resources, skills, talents, time, and facilities? To illustrate, a church located near a city once had several members who owned farms. Many children in a nearby inner city usually had only the city streets for play for the summer. A ready resource (the members who owned farms with "soil banked" land) made it relatively easy to accomplish the objective: "Get fifty city children into the fresh air next summer." Day camping on some of the soil bank acreage of church members' farms was soon a reality.

5. *What Is Your Church Doing Right Now?*

Some objectives may reflect programs already under way. It isn't necessary to stop such programs just because you have begun a planning process. If a new objective covers things you are presently doing, relate what is being done to the objective in each of the next phases of planning.

6. *Finances*

Funds may appear available to achieve an objective or could be made available if the program plan included fund raising in it.

7. *What Has Your Church Been Asked to Do?*

During interviews with community agencies and organiza-

Are we listening to what the community is telling us?

tions did any of them ask your church to take responsibility for specific projects? Does the objective reflect things your community has asked you to do?

8. *What's "In"?*

   Does the objective focus on issues or areas of concern about which your people are already enthusiastic and eager to do something, *right now?* Sometimes a short-term objective should be undertaken immediately to benefit from enthusiasm about what is crucial at the moment.

9. *What's Going On in Your Denomination?*

   Does the objective reflect any priorities you have heard about from your denomination? Perhaps your congregation should consider working on objectives being highlighted or suggested within its larger family.

10. *How Clear Are Your Criteria?*

    A good objective suggests its criteria—what the planner should look for, observe, count, or measure in some way as a basis for evaluation. (See page 67.) Does the objective point to criteria? Do you know what to look for as evidence that the change required by the objective has really taken place?

COMPLETING THE STEP OF SETTING PRIORITIES

When you have completed the task of testing all your objectives against these guidelines, each objective may have one or more guideline numbers written next to it. For each objective count how many guideline numbers it has, and write the count in the right-hand margin of the newsprint. Within each goal put the objectives in priority order according to the count each received. When a tie occurs, put the objective having more of the first three guideline numbers ahead of the other(s).

Bring each goal, with its related objectives in priority order, to the congregation for approval. Ask the congregation to approve the *goals,* using the objectives only as illustrations of what the goals imply. Actual objectives will be developed later.

Display your goals and objectives where they may be seen easily. Put them in your church bulletins, newsletters, and other media. Later, when your church accomplishes an objective, celebrate the occasion.

Preparation for Mission Design

First . . . *TAKE A BREAK!* Your Planning Task Force has just spent important time and energy completing Goal Development. Schedule no task force meetings for at least three weeks. Relax!

Second . . . During these weeks check with Planning Task Force members to see who will be able to continue to serve. You may need to replace some members. Now is a good time to bring replacements "on board" if they are needed.

The next diagram shows where you are in the planning process.

Phase III
Mission Design

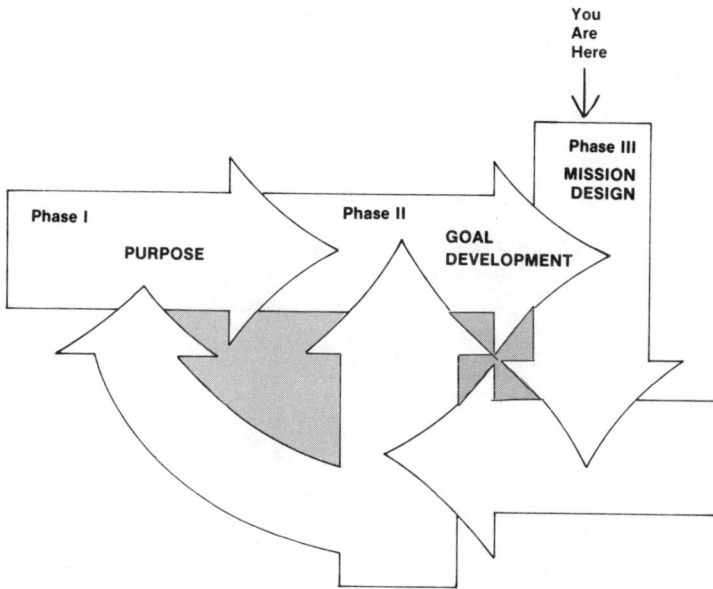

You
Are
Here

Phase III
**MISSION
DESIGN**

Phase I

PURPOSE

Phase II

**GOAL
DEVELOPMENT**

INTRODUCTION

STEP
3:0

You have now stated your Goals and their related priority Objectives. Objectives, however, don't just happen. Your task now is to design ways your church can best work to achieve its objectives.

A clearly defined objective will suggest a number of ways to reach it. We call these ways or methods *Program Plans* (some persons use the term "strategies"). Program Plans give you opportunities to work out new ways to get things done.

After you have created your *Program Plans,* the next step in Mission Design will be to develop *Program Plan Details* for each one.

PROGRAM PLANS

STEP 3:1 A Program Plan is *an overall blueprint describing in general how to use what you have to achieve each objective.* Most of your objectives can be achieved in a number of ways. Current ways of getting things done in your church may not always make the best use of your resources. This step involves picking the most promising way of reaching the objective for which you can prepare a blueprint.

The overall blueprint is a plan of action to help our church grow from where it is to where it should be.

In Step 3:1 you should explore as many ways as you can to work toward each objective. Look over these questions as you begin to develop Program Plans:

1. Who is the target audience?
   a. For whom is this objective intended?
   b. Who would be served by this objective if it were achieved?

2. Can we organize our congregation to reach this objective?
   a. Do we really have the "horses needed to pull this wagon"?
   b. What advance arrangements would we have to make if we decide to use this particular blueprint or Program Plan?
   c. Should we try to do this work by ourselves? Will we have to get help from some other group? If so, what kind and how much?
3. Can we motivate our church members to achieve this objective?
   a. Are we motivated to do what the objective challenges us to do?
   b. Will our congregation risk what is required by this objective?

Remember, each Program Plan describes *in general* a course of action that could be taken to reach a priority objective. A Program Plan indicates:

(1) principal actors (congregation, boards, committees, task forces); (2) particular responsibilities; and (3) the types of human and financial resources needed to carry out the action.

Some objectives may be so specific they indicate only one way that can be used to work toward them. If this is the case with any of your objectives, don't waste time trying to generate other possibilities just for the sake of having more than one Program Plan to consider. Begin to develop Program Plans for the objectives you ranked as *most important* in Step 2:10 of Goal Development.

WHO SHOULD DEVELOP PROGRAM PLANS

Here are three options for who should be involved in generating ideas for Program Plans.

Option 1. The Planning Task Force can work alone. However, others in the church may feel left out of the process.

Option 2. Identify the particular Program Plan categories the Planning Task Force hopes to cover at its next meeting. Invite to that meeting persons from boards, committees, or age groups related to categories you will discuss. Include them in your process.

Option 3. For each objective invite the board, committee, or other organized unit of the church which best fits the subject of that objective to develop the related Program Plan. The

Planning Task Force's job would be to coordinate the development of all Program Plans. If a unit is not represented on the Planning Task Force, a task force member could be asked to work with the unit while it is developing the Program Plan.

Your community probably has resource persons, such as area ministers, other denominational staff persons, seminary and university faculty, local community organizers, etc. These persons can help you expand the number of your Program Plan possibilities. They can assist you under any of the three options.

HOW TO DEVELOP PROGRAM PLANS

Write one objective statement at the top of each sheet of newsprint. Brainstorm for five to fifteen minutes possible ways to achieve the objective. Encourage your people to say what pops into their minds for each objective. Be open and creative. Don't stop to analyze any of the suggested ideas or to discuss details. Let the ideas flow. Be different. Be daring.

Write on newsprint every idea, dream, and hope that your group suggests. Don't limit yourself because of high costs, lack of staff, or lack of facilities. Don't hesitate to suggest what might, at first, appear to be "way out" ideas.

At the conclusion of your brainstorming session you will probably have many ideas on the newsprint sheets. Sort out the ideas you feel are most meaningful and usable for your church and community. Try combining some ideas to build a Program Plan. Work with various combinations of ideas until a plan emerges about which the group can be enthusiastic.

A word of caution. You may have difficulty listing Program Plan ideas for certain objectives. If this happens, there are three things you can do:

1. You can assign to someone the job of developing a Program Plan. This work could then be brought back to the group for reaction.
2. You might contact denominational staff for suggestions.
3. You may have to set aside an objective if, after some exploration, there seems to be no possible way for your church to pursue it.

AN EXAMPLE OF PROGRAM PLANS[1]

The following example uses the category and objective presented earlier on page 65.

Category A: Developing spiritually vital members.

> *Objective: Short Term*—Within two months, our congregation will officially adopt a common definition for the terms "active members" and "inactive members."
>
> *Program Plan:* Ask the diaconate to define terms and get the congregation to vote on them.

PREPARING PROGRAM PLAN DETAILS

| STEP 3:2 |

Individual parts of a Program Plan are called Program Plan Details. The following questions will help you identify what should be included as details of a Program Plan:

1. *What* is the *Objective* and its related *Program Plan?*
2. *Who* will be involved in making this happen?
3. *When* will this happen?
   (When will the events of the program begin?)
   (When will they be finished?)
4. *Where* will this happen?
   (And, under what conditions?)
5. *How* will this happen?
   (What will persons *do* to make this happen?)
6. *What* specifically will be different or changed if what happens is successful?
   (Be sure to relate this to your criteria. See pages 67-68.)

Program Plan Details provide a complete description of: (1) what is to be done; (2) who will be involved; (3) what their specific assignments are; (4) the target dates when their work will begin and be completed, and the dates when progress reports are to be made; and (5) the changes that are intended.

Think of a Program Plan as an architect's sketches and pictures. Consider Program Plan Details as the blueprints which explain just how to build. They show everyone involved what to do and when.

---

[1] Other examples may be found on pages 55-57 in LCPM.

A building project requires a detailed set of blueprints and a construction schedule. In the same way program planning requires specific descriptions of activities and a schedule for doing what is planned.

When you are ready to work on Program Plan Details, decide first *who* will be the Program Plan Manager.[2] Invite this person to develop the Program Plan Details for review by the Planning Task Force. The best Program Plan can fail if the leaders responsible for it do not understand it or are not committed to it. Having the leaders develop the Program Plan Details is a good way to avoid later misunderstandings or a lack of commitment.

Program Plan Managers should consider these guidelines when working out their Program Plan Details:

1. Be realistic about the time your church will need to carry out the details of a Program Plan.
2. Maintain direct communications with others who will be involved in carrying out the Program Plan Details.
3. Be realistic about the dollars required by each detail of the Program Plan, including both direct and hidden costs.
4. Create a blueprint, the detailed guidelines to help you carry out the plan.
5. Be careful not to skip details. Double-check each one.
6. Provide guidance for any others sharing in your Program Plan Details to know where to get help if they need it.
7. Plan to collect evaluation facts as you go along so you can measure your progress during and at the conclusion of the Program Plan. Refer to Phase V, $\boxed{\text{Step 5:2}}$ for the tools needed to collect your facts.
8. Decide how often you will compare your evaluation facts with the Objective to see if the Program Plan Details are doing what they were designed to do.
9. Make sure that you as Program Plan Manager know from the start: (1) when to make both progress reports and the final evaluation report; and (2) the reporting procedures to be used.

Newsprint can be used when developing your Program Plan Details. Write the Objective at the top of the sheet; then state the

---

[2] See $\boxed{\text{STEP 4:1}}$, Program Plan Manager, on page 84.

Program Plan as you have developed it in Step 3:1

The following example uses the Category, Objective, and Program Plan listed on page 77. The details answer the questions found on page 77 and follow the form of the Sample Worksheet shown on page 81.

AN EXAMPLE OF PROGRAM PLAN DETAILS[3]

Category A: Developing spiritually vital church members.

1. *Objective: Short Term*—Within two months, our congregation will officially adopt a common definition for the terms "active members" and "inactive members."

   Program Plan: Ask the diaconate to define terms and get the congregation to vote on them.

2. *Who will make this happen?*

   (a) The Program Plan Manager will begin the process by inviting the diaconate to take responsibility for this Program Plan.

   (b) The diaconate will consider the invitation and, if it accepts, will submit its work to the church moderator.

   (c) The church moderator and/or the pastor will call a church business meeting and preside over it.

   (d) The congregation will decide.

3. *When will this happen?*

   The definitions should be ready by   (date)   . The congregational vote should take place by   (date)   .

4. *Where will this happen?*

   At the next meeting of the diaconate, to be held at John Smith's home, and at the   (date)   business meeting of our church.

5. *How will this happen?*

   (a) The diaconate will ask the church clerk to provide copies of church membership policies and church actions about membership for its study.

   (b) The diaconate will prepare its definitions and give them to

---

[3] Other examples may be found on pages 72-76 of LCPM.

the church moderator at least two weeks before the church business meeting.

(c) The church moderator and/or the pastor by (date) will call a congregational meeting to vote on the diaconate's report and will share the proposed definitions at least a week ahead.

(d) The moderator will preside over the congregational meeting where one hour will be allocated for discussion and/or debate before the vote. Voting will be by secret ballot.

6. *What will be different?*

We will have a clear distinction between those who are active members and those who are not. We will be able to challenge those now inactive, to inform any who wish to know what is meant by active membership in our church, and to design Program Plans that depend on our knowing just how many active members we have for possible support of the plans.

REVIEWING PROGRAM PLAN DETAILS

| STEP 3:3 | Each program Plan Manager should present a copy of the completed Program Plan Details to the Planning Task Force for its review. The Planning Task Force is |

responsible to see that each proposed set of Program Plan Details is complete and fits the intention of the Objective and the Program Plan. The Program Plan Details worksheet should then be returned to the Program Plan Manager after the Planning Task Force has approved it.

(Sample Worksheet)

PROGRAM PLAN DETAILS

Category: _____

1. Objective: _____

Program Plan: _____

_____

_____

2. *Who* will be involved in making this happen?

_____

3. *When* will this happen? (Start? Finish?)

_____

4. *Where* will this happen?

_____

5. *How* will this happen? (What will persons *do* to make this happen?)

_____

_____

_____

6. *What* specifically *will be different or changed* if "what happens" is successful?
(Relate to your criteria.)

_____

_____

Date written: _____ By whom: _____

Approved by: _____ Date: _____

Phase IV
Mission Management

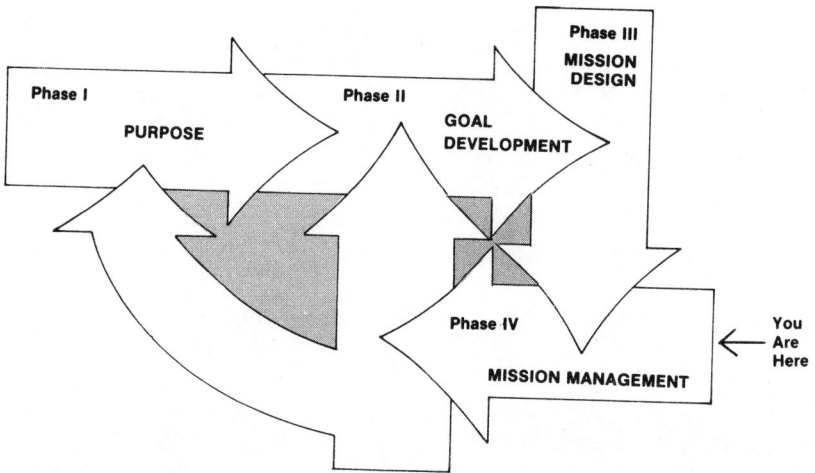

Phase III
MISSION
DESIGN

Phase I

PURPOSE

Phase II

GOAL
DEVELOPMENT

Phase IV

MISSION MANAGEMENT

You
Are
Here

INTRODUCTION

STEP 4:0 Successful planners are the ones who "plan their work and work their plans." In Phase I through Phase III you have built your plan. Your *plan* is now your tool for action. Your plan, however, is not a machine which will run itself.

Translating your vision (your Program Plan) into action requires managers. Managers are people who get things done. Managers are people who keep their vision in mind while giving attention to details. Program Plan Details require close attention if they are to be used to move people toward their chosen objective.

Mission Management has two levels:

1. Management of each Objective and its Program Plan.
2. Management of the entire set of Program Plans.

Program Plan Managers are needed to handle the first level, each managing a Program Plan and its details. A Program Coordinator is needed to handle the second level, coordinating the work of all Program Plan Managers.

PROGRAM PLAN MANAGER

STEP 4:1

Each Program Plan should have its own manager. Each Program Plan Manager, working with others, is responsible *to design* and carry out his or her Program Plan Details, *to monitor* what is happening, *to make* progress reports to the Program Coordinator, and *to submit* a final evaluation report through the Program Coordinator to the Planning Task Force.

PROGRAM PLAN MANAGERS SHOULD:

1. Understand and be committed to the planning process you are using.
2. Be committed to the Objective and its Program Plan.
3. Develop the Program Plan Details and submit them to the Planning Task Force for approval.
4. Carry out the Program Plan Details, as approved.
5. Use the details in the plan to check progress in terms of people who should be involved, deadlines that should be met, actions that should be taken, and counts that should be recorded to see if intended changes are taking place.[1]
6. Submit periodic reports to the Program Coordinator. If problems occur, contact the Program Coordinator without delay.

---

[1] For numbers 5 and 9 use the Evaluation Worksheet and the Record of Results Worksheet described in Phase V, pages 86 and 88 in LCPM.

7. Make recommendations to the Program Coordinator whenever the Program Plan Details should be revised because conditions have changed.
8. At all times be able to distinguish between what *is* taking place as compared with what was *intended* to take place.
9. Prepare an evaluation report for the Program Coordinator to use with the Planning Task Force and the congregation when the Program Plan is completed.

WHO CAN BE A PROGRAM PLAN MANAGER?

The Program Plan Manager could be:
1. A member of the Planning Task Force.
2. A member of a board, committee, council, or other group you think should be responsible for a Program Plan.
3. Someone from your congregation suited to manage a particular Program Plan.

PROGRAM COORDINATOR

| STEP 4:2 |

Name a Program Coordinator to whom your Program Plan Managers can relate. Program Plan Managers need someone to whom they can give progress reports with some confidence that the big picture of your church's total ministry will not become blurred by all the necessary detail work.

THE PROGRAM COORDINATOR SHOULD:

1. Understand and be committed to the planning process you are using.
2. Provide orientation for each new Program Plan Manager about how his or her Program Plan is related to all the other Program Plans.
3. Receive reports from and provide guidance to Program Plan Managers.
4. Make periodic reports to the Planning Task Force on progress of all Program Plans under way.
5. Through the church newsletter or other media share with the congregation the progress and/or changes for your church's total program.

6. Review with the Planning Task Force every six months all of the Program Plans being managed to determine whether all categories for your Areas of Concern (see pages 53-54) are covered by what your church is currently doing.
7. Assist the Planning Task Force to keep on target with its priority objectives awaiting the appointment of a Program Plan Manager.
8. Help each Program Plan Manager present the final evaluation report to the Planning Task Force.

WHO CAN BE THE PROGRAM COORDINATOR?

The Program Coordinator could be:

1. The chairperson of your Planning Task Force, a logical choice if that person is willing to serve.

Name a program coordinator to whom your program plan managers can relate.

2. Your pastor, even though his or her work is already time-consuming and comprehensive. (This is a particularly good choice if the congregation, in fact, gives high priority to planning.)
3. A person in your congregation whose skills and experiences make him or her suited for this kind of work. (Add this person to the Planning Task Force.)

SUMMARY

Mission Management is both the Program Coordinator's job and the Program Plan Manager's job. Mission Management turns plans into results. Persons who manage your planning operation are the leaders, who, with patience and gentle firmness, can help your church translate its vision (goals and objectives) into action with successful outcomes.

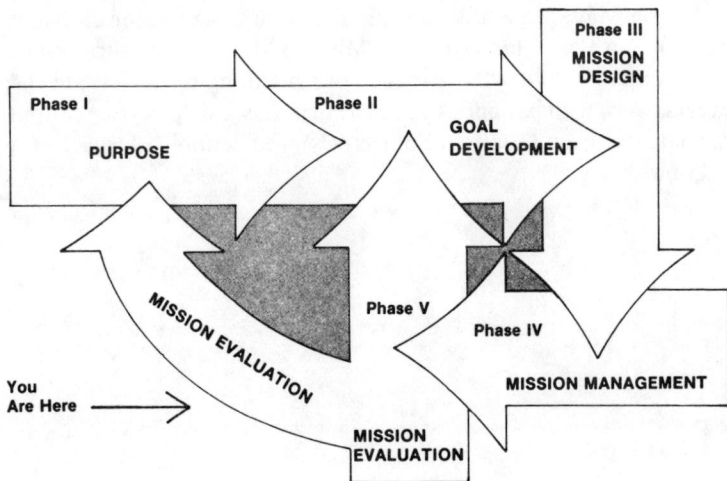

Phase I

PURPOSE

Phase II

GOAL
DEVELOPMENT

Phase III
MISSION
DESIGN

MISSION EVALUATION

Phase V

Phase IV

MISSION MANAGEMENT

You
Are Here →

MISSION
EVALUATION

Phase V
Mission Evaluation

INTRODUCTION

Evaluation means *considering carefully the worth or "value" of what you have done.* Evaluating programs makes it possible to answer:

- What happened?
- Was it what we wanted?
- Did enough happen to make our work worthwhile?
- What did we do best?
- What would it have been better to do differently?

The Program Plan Manager, with assistance from the Program Coordinator, is responsible for evaluation. These two must cooperate for evaluation to be successful.

The Program Plan Manager will know best what the Program Plan Details require and how the related criteria fit the Objective. In addition, the Program Plan Manager will be involved in preparing progress reports used to assess how well the Program Plan is moving along. Finally, the Program Plan Manager (or someone he or she assigns) will observe, collect notes, hand out and receive questionnaires, and do whatever else is needed to gather and interpret the facts necessary for evaluation.

The Program Coordinator is responsible for receiving progress reports and for working with each Program Plan Manager in preparing the final evaluation report. All evaluation reports should be forwarded by the Program Coordinator to the Planning Task Force.

Program evaluation has five steps:

Step 5:1 reviews pre-evaluation activities you completed in Phases II, III, IV.

Step 5:2 describes *structure, process,* and *product* as a way to organize your evaluation work.

Step 5:3 provides guidance for preparing facts to use in evaluation.

Step 5:4 describes ways to report conclusions from your facts and ways to make recommendations based on them.

Step 5:5 suggests how to build the Big Picture.

PRE-EVALUATION ACTIVITIES

STEP 5:1

This planning process calls for some pre-evaluation activities in earlier Phases. These are beginning points for Mission Evaluation and are reviewed below.

In **Phase II** | Step 2:9 |, you worked on your objective statements using the ideas that an objective: (1) is a target, (2) is derived from a goal statement, and (3) is worded so movement toward it can be measured.

On pages 67-68 you were asked to get your Objectives ready for use in evaluation by writing criteria for each one—to name what exactly was expected or intended by each Objective. You were asked to decide what should be looked for, observed, counted, or measured in some way as clues or signs (criteria) of: (1) what had been achieved and (2) how well the Program Plan helped to achieve these ends.

In | Step 2:10 | you set priorities among your Objectives. Priority guideline #10 (page 71) asked you to consider how clearly each Objective pointed to the clues or signs which should be looked for as evidence of achievement.

In **Phase III** | Step 3:2 |. Program Plan Managers were instructed to describe *who* were to be involved, *when, where,* and *how;* also *what* would be different or changed if the Program Plan Details were carried out successfully. These descriptions were to be written on worksheets like the one on page 81 for review and approval by the Planning Task Force.

In **Phase IV** | Step 4:1 |, Program Plan Managers were given certain pre-evaluation responsibilities (as part of a total list of responsibilities, numbers correspond to total list):

5. Use the details in the plan to check progress in terms of people who should be involved, deadlines that should be met, actions that should be taken, and counts that should be recorded to see if intended changes are taking place.

8. At all times be able to distinguish between what *is* taking place as compared with what was *intended* to take place.

In Step 4:2 Program Coordinators were asked (among other things) to:

3. Receive reports from and provide guidance to Program Plan Managers.

4. Make periodic reports to the Planning Task Force on the progress of all Program Plans under way.

If you carried out these suggestions, you now have material useful for evaluating your Program Plan and its details. Step 5:2 presents a way to organize this evaluation material.

ORGANIZE YOUR EVALUATION WORK

STEP 5:2 In this planning process, you need to evaluate three elements:

ELEMENT 1: How well did you organize to get the job done? This element is called *"structure evaluation."* It deals with the arrangements you make in order to be able to carry out your Program Plan Details. Jesus pointed to this element when He observed that no person plans to build without first sitting down to figure out what it will cost (Luke 14:28, TEV).

We might well ask: "What happened to people because of the planning process?"

91

ELEMENT 2: How well did things go? We call this element *"process evaluation."* It deals with the actions you took in carrying out your Program Plan Details. It deals with the kinds of things to which Proverbs 4:26 (TEV) refers, "Plan carefully what you do, . . ."

ELEMENT 3: What changed? We call this element *"product evaluation."* It deals with what comes about as the result of having carried out your Program Plan Details. The New Testament makes several references to this element: "you will know them by their fruits" (Matthew 7:16); "The fruit of the Spirit is love, joy, peace, patience, kindness, goodness, faithfulness, gentleness, self-control" (Galatians 5:22-23); " . . . if it bears fruit . . . well and good; but if not, you can cut it down" (Luke 13:9).

Use these three elements—*structure, process,* and *product*—to organize your evaluation work. This will build a string of evidence between the intention stated in your Objective and the results you achieved from carrying out your Program Plan. The logic of such organization goes something like this:

1. If the *structure* evaluation shows you made the proper arrangements to carry out your process; and
2. If the *process* evaluation shows the steps you planned to take were, in fact, taken and in their proper order;
3. Then there is good reason to assume that what happened, the *product*, was related to what you did.

STRUCTURE EVALUATION

The evaluation of *structure* asks the question "How well did we organize to get the job done?" Your Program Plan Details show what arrangements you *intended* to set up to carry out your program, i.e., the structure you planned to use. For example, if your program was to help persons learn to bake a cake, the structure questions would deal with the kitchen, the stove, the cooking utensils, the recipe books, etc.

Check your filled-in Evaluation Worksheet (page 94) against the *who, when,* and *where* described in your Program Plan Details:
Were the right people in the right place at the right time with the proper tools and materials so they could take the steps described in the Program Plan Details?

Structure evaluation is asking:
"How well did we use our buildings, equipment and resource persons to get the job done?"

PROCESS EVALUATION

Process evaluation is the next step after the evaluation of structure. Go back to the example of helping someone learn how to bake a cake. The process questions would be, "Did the people *know which* recipe to follow?" "Did they *know how* to follow the recipe?" *"Did* they follow the recipe?" Evaluating the process described in your Program Plan Details changes these questions only a little.

Check your Evaluation Worksheet against the *how* described in your Program Plan Details. Ask such questions as:
- How well did the persons involved know the blueprint of the Program Plan Details?
- Were steps in the Program Plan Details set in proper order, so persons could follow them?
- Did each step take place at the right time?
- Did anyone get mixed up? (Try to find out *why* whenever this type of thing happens.)

Key Steps in Local Church Planning

EVALUATION WORKSHEET

Goal: _____

1. Objective: _____

   Program Plan: _____

List specifics as described in your Program Plan Details	What really took place?	If you had to make adjustments from what was planned, what were they? Why were they necessary?
2. Who will be involved?		
3. When will this happen?		
4. Where will this happen?		
5. How will this happen?		
6. What will be different if this happens?	(Use RECORD OF RESULTS Worksheet.)	

PRODUCT EVALUATION

Product evaluation is the final step after you have evaluated structure and process. Again, consider the example of teaching someone to bake a cake. The product questions would be: "Did the cake look appetizing?" "Did it taste good?"

Begin your product evaluation with what you have written on the Record of Results Worksheet, mentioned first on page 84 and shown below. The left side will be filled in with what you have written under Question #6 on your Program Plan Details Worksheet. The right side should be filled in by the time you complete Phase IV, Mission Management. What is written becomes your record of (1) what you *planned to achieve* through the program and (2) what was *actually achieved* through your Mission Management.

Evaluate the product of your Program Plan by comparing (or contrasting) what is written on the right-hand side of your Record of Results with what is written on the left. If the two sides are alike, you have probably reached your Objective. If they are not alike, you will be able to see how far you fell below, or went beyond, your Objective.

RECORD OF RESULTS WORKSHEET
(Completes item #6 of Evaluation Worksheet)

WHAT WE INTEND TO HAPPEN		WHAT DID HAPPEN	
What change do we want? (outcome or result)	What clues or signs will be used to show this change? (criteria)	What clues or signs did we see?	How much of each sign did we see?

PREPARING FACTS FOR EVALUATION

STEP 5:3

This step has three parts:
1. Defining the facts you need for evaluation;
2. Putting those facts into order;
3. Finding out what this arrangement of facts means.

DEFINING THE NEEDED FACTS

There are two ways to find out things about people. First, you can look at them (observe or measure). Second, you can ask them questions (interview, survey, test). Your design for collecting evaluation facts will be one or the other of these two ways, or some combination of both.

Evaluation is deciding how well you accomplished what was intended when you wrote your objective.

There are three kinds of evaluation facts:
1. Facts about understandings
   —an understanding is something a person has learned, what the person knows and is able to use;
2. Facts about attitudes
   —an attitude is how a person feels about something. It is usually shown through a gesture, a facial expression, a spoken opinion, a tone of voice;
3. Facts about actions
   —actions are the ways people go about doing things. Sometimes

an action shows a new skill or an increase in an already existing skill. It may show a habit is increasing or decreasing. It may show a change in custom, method, or practice.

There are four levels at which facts can be gathered:
1. "Nominal" facts
   These are facts that name. They indicate only whether a thing is present or absent. An example is the numbers on football players' uniforms. The numbers identify the players so that the fans can tell whether a particular individual is on the bench or on the playing field. Nominal facts are numbers that "name."
2. "Ordinal" facts
   These facts let you put things into ranks: first, second, third, and so on.

   To put things into ranks simply means to set in order on some basis of "bigger than"—"smaller than," without having to say exactly what "bigger" or "smaller" may mean.

   A typical example is an elementary school teacher's process of lining up the class for a group photograph. Though the teacher doesn't use a yardstick or a tape measure, he or she has no difficulty putting the tall people in the back row and the short people in the front row.

   Ordinal facts allow persons to make real distinctions without having to be precise about the degree of the distinction.
3. "Interval" facts
   These facts allow you not only to put things into ranks, but you can also describe equal differences between ranks. Interval facts, however, have no way to define what zero means, and no good idea of infinity.

   An example of this is the thermometer a mother uses to take her baby's temperature. The thermometer has no zero point (it would be meaningless for the baby to have a temperature of zero). The thermometer has no infinitely hot point (the baby is not in the middle of the sun). But within these limits the mother knows that each mark on the thermometer is the same distance from the next mark, and she can use the thermometer to tell whether the baby's temperature is normal or whether the baby is running a fever. We find interval facts used in measures of human knowledge or

understanding and in various of the tests of mental abilities.
4. "Ratio" facts
These facts are the kind bankers use.

Bankers' numbers have a true zero point: you can be in debt to the bank (be below the zero point); you can have a bank account (have money deposited against which you can write checks); you can have no money in the bank (be right at the zero point).

Bankers' numbers have equal intervals; ten dollars is twice as much as five dollars and one-half as much as twenty.

Bankers' numbers also suggest some working idea of infinity, such as "all the money ever made between creation and the end of the world."

Most church Program Plan evaluations will involve nominal and ordinal facts. Some Program Plans, those involving the work of trustees or persons in stewardship projects, will use ratio level facts. Some church education programs may use interval-type facts.

When gathering facts and figures about understandings, attitudes, and actions, be sensitive to the level at which you are collecting these facts. This will help both those who have the responsibility to observe (or ask questions) and those who are responsible to interpret what the observers record.

Be careful that from the start you know how you are going to use the facts you collect. Do not gather merely interesting facts and figures. A good way to make sure you are collecting useful facts is to tie what is being collected to a specific sign or clue used as part of the criteria related to the Objective for the Program Plan.

PUTTING YOUR FACTS INTO ORDER

After you have recorded your facts and figures, you may be facing several piles of paper. These piles must be reduced to some pattern that has meaning. Mainly, this means putting the facts and figures about the same event onto the same sheet of paper (or stapling pages together if several sheets are involved).

If you asked questions for which persons composed their own answers (open-end questions), all answers to the same question should be put on one sheet of paper. Then mark which open-end answers are positive, which are negative, and which are neutral. Next to each answer put some facts that identify the type of person giving the answer (such as age, sex, church leadership responsibility, occupation, grade in school, etc.). This will allow you to recognize similarities and differences among the several types of people usually involved in each Program Plan.

You may ask questions to which persons respond by checking one or more answers that you provide (closed-end questions). These answers are easier to reduce into a usable form. Record these answers on a tally sheet listing each type of person answering (man/woman, youth/adult, regular attender/infrequent attender, and so on).

When open-end answers are put into categories, such as "Strongly Agree," "Agree," "Neutral," "Disagree," "Strongly Disagree," the answers can be coded in the same way as closed-end answers. For each question, sort all coded answers into separate piles according to the types of people or their answers; if needed, combine them into other piles, and count each pile.

For example, the sheets of paper could first be separated between those marked "Male" and those marked "Female." Then each of these two piles could be further sorted between those marking "Yes" and those marking "No" as the answer to a given question. The result of these two "sorts," when counted, would be: (1) the number of "Males" saying "Yes," (2) those saying "No." (3) the number of "Females" saying "Yes," and (4) those saying "No." Such two-way sorts show any differences in the way persons of different sexes answer questions.

The important thing is that your facts, once you have put them into order, should be "captured" in some way to make it possible to separate or to combine and to count the facts you have collected.

FINDING WHAT THESE FACTS MEAN

Now you need to find out what you found out. What things are alike? What things are different? What does it all mean?

This planning process identifies four ways to look at your facts, depending on the level at which they were collected (nominal, ordinal, interval, ratio). The first three ways are generally no more complicated than proving your monthly bank statement. The fourth is more complicated. Most church Program Plan evaluations will use only the first two ways. Some Program Plan evaluations need the third and fourth also.

We call the four *counting, figuring, computing,* and *calculating.* The first two are fairly easy. The third is not much more difficult than following the special recipe for your favorite cake. The fourth requires someone trained in mathematics. But there are more and more of these people around, and some of them are active Christians. They would gladly volunteer their skills if local churches gave them an opportunity to do so.

In addition, many low-cost, hand-held calculators have special keys to do automatic calculation of such things as square roots. The time in church program evaluation is at hand for using mathematics to find out what your facts mean. Many elementary schools introduce students to hand-held calculators. Most high schools assume the use of calculators as a basic tool for math and science courses. Your able young people may be willing to help you find out what your evaluation facts mean.

Counting—the easiest way to find meaning in your facts.

Counting is a skill all of us use. Many persons in their work use a tally system to take inventories. They use four vertical marks with a diagonal line to indicate 5 (as, ╫╫). The count of these fives multiplied by five gives the total or sum. This simple device is a powerful observation tool for marking the increase or decrease of a sign or clue.

Another type of counting involves the "median"—the middle number in a list that has been put into a ranked order (see page 97). Half of the numbers in the list will be above the median, and half below.

A third kind of counting deals with the "mode," the category which has the most tallies of all categories being examined. For example, if "Strongly Agree" has twelve tallies and all other categories have fewer, then "Strongly Agree" is the mode.

Using tallies, sums, medians, and modes requires nothing more than paper and pencil. The only mathematics used is addition. (Counting tally sets by fives, i.e., 5-10-15-20-etc., is easier for some persons than multiplying; do it either way—you will get the same answer.)

Figuring—not quite as easy as counting, but almost.

Figuring includes:
- graphs
- charts
- percents
- the average (the "mean," the sum of all scores divided by the number of scores being added)
- ratios (a way of relating one thing to another using simple fractions)

Most junior high school math books give instructions on how to use these figuring tools. A handy book for adults who have been out of school for a while is *Mathematics for Practical Use, A Simplified Guide,* by Kaj L. Nielsen. It is available in paperback (Barnes and Noble, Inc., Everyday Handbooks No. 212).

Computing—a little more difficult than figuring; get one of your able high school students to help.

Computing involves arranging facts into patterns (known as "arrays") by scores, ranks, or categories. Once facts are in an array, you can compute the difference between averages, the relationship between two groups, and the likelihood that a trend may exist.

For your use (or that of the high school student) we suggest two helpful pamphlets issued by the Union College Character Research Project.

These pamphlets give simple recipes for finding out what your facts mean. They were designed for use by lay persons in local churches. One pamphlet is *Basic Tools for Creative Research, Designed for the Layman to Use in Solving Everyday Problems in an Objective Way.* The second pamphlet is *Data Analysis, Statistical and Technical Aids.* Each pamphlet can be purchased for less than $2.50 by writing to: Character Research Project, 207 State St., Schenectady, NY 12305.

Calculating—Is there an engineer in your congregation? An insurance actuary? A high school math teacher? A sociologist? Someone who just likes mathematics?

Calculating involves advanced mathematical skills. It includes variance analysis, factor analysis, multiple regression analysis, etc. Many churches have members whose occupations require them to work with mathematics at the calculating level. If you know of such persons, this part of your evaluation work can allow them to use their talents for the church in a new way.

Each Program Plan Manager should put his or her evaluation facts together. Use the *kinds of facts, levels of facts,* and *ways to arrange them* which best fit the Program Plan Details. When this work is completed, the Program Plan Manager is ready for $\boxed{\text{Step 5:4}}$.

REPORTING CONCLUSIONS
AND RECOMMENDATIONS

$\boxed{\begin{array}{c}\textbf{STEP}\\\textbf{5:4}\end{array}}$ Evaluation involves reporting conclusions and recommendations based on facts and figures you have collected, reduced, and studied. It is the way church planners make decisions about future Program Plans.

You are now ready to draw conclusions, using what you have learned from your evaluation facts.

- Did we make the right arrangements? (structure)
- Did we take the right steps? (process)
- Did we achieve the intended result? (product)

Your evaluation report should include the answers to these three questions. In this way you are accounting for your stewardship of resources used in the Program Plan.

Your evaluation report should also include your recommendation concerning the future of the Program Plan. Your recommendation may be one of four types:

- Repeat, because . . .
- Revise, because . . .
- Replace, because . . .
- Stop, because . . .

Complete the appropriate sentence for the type of recommendation you make. Give your evaluation report to the Program Coordinator for use by the Planning Task Force at its next meeting.

THE BIG PICTURE

$\boxed{\begin{array}{c}\textbf{STEP}\\\textbf{5:5}\end{array}}$ Over a period of time the Planning Task Force will receive several Program Plan evaluation reports whose Objectives come from the same goal. When looked at together, these reports from Program Plan Managers will begin to build a big picture showing movement toward one Goal.

In addition, your church probably has several Program Plans under way, which are related to different Goals. At least once a year the Planning Task Force should look at all Goals for which Program Plan evaluation reports have been received. By examining recommendations related to Objectives for all of the Goals, the Planning Task Force can begin building a bigger picture of how well the church's life expresses what is said in its Purpose Statement.

As we compare what our church is doing with what our purpose statement says, we will be in a position to reexamine the statement itself.

When you have worked through several evaluations in this planning cycle, you will probably want to review your Goals and Objectives. From time to time you may even want to rephrase your Purpose Statement. Moving through a series of planning cycles does not mean just doing the same tasks over again but planning on the basis of new information, new insights, and new skills gained by following this Planning Process.

A Second Cycle
of Planning

A local church Planning Task Force should periodically recycle certain planning ⏐ Steps ⏐ . It should return to ⏐ Step 2:6 ⏐ and review assumptions at least every three years. All later steps in the planning process would then be followed, based on any changes made in the assumptions.

At least every six years the Planning Task Force should return to ⏐ Step 2:3 ⏐ and update the data gathered about the church, the community, and the world. In light of these new data, a new

The planning process needs to be a continuing part of church life.

Information Summary can be prepared and later planning steps taken. Needless to say, the second time around will likely be less time-consuming.

As you become familiar with this planning process, it will be easier to use. Through planning, may God guide you to a challenging future in which your church is more effective by

- Stating your purpose
- Writing your Goals and Objectives
- Developing your Program Plans (and details)
- Managing your mission
- Evaluating your progress.

For Your Notes

For Your Notes

For Your Notes

For Your Notes

For Your Notes

For Your Notes